Preface

In an era where technology is rapidly transforming every facet of our lives, Cloud Computing and the Internet of Things (IoT) stand at the forefront of this digital revolution. These technologies have not only reshaped the way we store, manage, and process data but have also paved the way for smart, connected devices that are becoming increasingly integral to our everyday experiences. As such, mastering the concepts and applications of Cloud Computing and IoT is essential for students and professionals who aspire to thrive in the evolving tech landscape.

This book, " **IGNOU Cloud Computing and IoT Previous Years Solved Papers,"** is specifically designed to support students enrolled in Indira Gandhi National Open University (IGNOU) as they prepare for their examinations. The book offers a comprehensive collection of solved questions from past exams, providing students with detailed solutions and explanations that enhance their understanding of key concepts.

Key Features of This Book:

- **Thorough Solutions:** Each question is accompanied by a detailed solution, explaining the step-by-step process to arrive at the correct answer. This helps students not only to learn the correct answers but also to understand the underlying principles and logic.
- **Comprehensive Coverage:** The book covers a wide range of topics within Cloud Computing and IoT, reflecting the breadth of the IGNOU curriculum. This ensures that students are well-prepared for any question they may encounter in their exams.
- **Enhanced Learning:** By working through these solved questions, students can reinforce their learning and gain insights into how to approach similar questions in the future. The explanations are designed to clarify complex concepts and provide practical examples where applicable.
- **Exam-Oriented Preparation:** The questions are selected from previous years' exams, giving students a realistic idea of the types of questions that are likely to appear in their upcoming exams. This targeted preparation helps students to focus their studies effectively.
- **Confidence Building:** Having access to solved questions boosts students' confidence as they approach their exams, knowing they have a reliable resource to help them review and solidify their knowledge.

This book is intended to be more than just a collection of answers; it is a learning tool that guides students through the intricacies of Cloud Computing and IoT. By engaging with the solved questions, students will not only prepare for their exams but also develop a deeper understanding of how these technologies function and how they can be applied in real-world scenarios.

We hope that this book will serve as a valuable companion for students as they navigate their studies and prepare to excel in their examinations. It is our belief that the knowledge and skills gained from this book will empower students to succeed not only in their academic pursuits but also in their future careers in the ever-expanding field of technology.

Table of Contents

MCS – 227
Master Of Computer Applications (MCA)
Chapter 1: Term-End Examination, June, 2022
MCS-227: Cloud Computing and IoT

Time: 3 Hours
Maximum Marks: 100
Weightage: 70
Note: Question No. 1 is compulsory. Answer any three Questions from the rest.

1. (a) Define Cloud Computing. List and explain the four categories of cloud deployment models. 10

Ans: Cloud computing is a technology that allows users to access and store data and applications over the internet instead of on a local computer or server. It enables on-demand access to shared resources, including servers, storage, databases, networking, software, and more, which can be rapidly provisioned and released with minimal management effort.

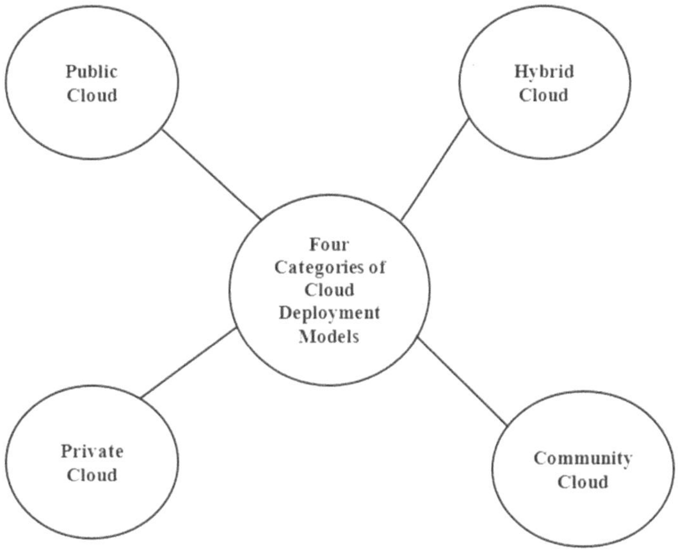

Four Categories of Cloud Deployment Models:

1. Public Cloud:

Definition: The public cloud is a cloud deployment model where the services and infrastructure are provided by a third-party cloud service provider and made available to the general public over the internet.

Explanation: In a public cloud, resources such as servers, storage, and applications are owned and operated by a cloud provider like Amazon Web Services (AWS), Microsoft Azure, or Google Cloud Platform (GCP). These resources are shared among multiple users (tenants), which helps in reducing costs. The public cloud is typically used for non-sensitive, high-volume workloads where cost efficiency and scalability are important.

2. Private Cloud:

Definition: A private cloud is a cloud deployment model that is dedicated to a single organization, offering more control over resources and data security.

Explanation: In a private cloud, the infrastructure is either hosted on-premises or by a third-party provider but is dedicated exclusively to one organization. This model is preferred by organizations that require strict security, compliance, and governance, such as financial institutions and government agencies. Private clouds can offer more customization and control but may require significant investments in hardware and maintenance.

3. Hybrid Cloud:

Definition: The hybrid cloud is a cloud deployment model that combines the use of both public and private clouds, allowing data and applications to be shared between them.

Explanation: A hybrid cloud environment allows an organization to leverage the benefits of both public and private clouds. For example, an organization might use a private cloud for sensitive data and applications that require tight security and compliance, while utilizing a public cloud for less critical operations and scalable workloads. The hybrid approach provides greater flexibility, optimized costs, and the ability to move workloads between clouds as needed.

4. Community Cloud:

Definition: A community cloud is a cloud deployment model where the cloud infrastructure is shared among several organizations that have common concerns, such as security, compliance, or specific business requirements.

Explanation: In a community cloud, multiple organizations with similar needs and goals share the cloud infrastructure. This model is often used by industries or groups with specific requirements, such as healthcare organizations or educational institutions, which may have similar regulatory or compliance needs. The community cloud provides a middle ground between the public and private cloud, offering some of the benefits of both, such as shared costs and enhanced security.

These deployment models offer different levels of control, scalability, and flexibility, depending on the specific needs of the organization.

Link https://youtu.be/bfzwKQq0TWU

QR Code:

(b) Define resource sharing in cloud computing. Explain the implementation of single-tenancy and multi-tenancy types of resource sharing in cloud computing. 10

Ans: Resource sharing in cloud computing refers to the ability to provide and allocate computing resources,such as processing power, storage, and network bandwidth,among multiple users or tenants. These resources are pooled together and dynamically allocated to users based on their demands, allowing for efficient utilization of the underlying infrastructure. Resource sharing is a fundamental aspect of cloud computing that enables scalability, cost-efficiency, and flexibility.

Implementation of Single-Tenancy and Multi-Tenancy Resource Sharing:

1. Single-Tenancy:

Definition: Single-tenancy is a cloud architecture model where a single instance of a software application and its associated resources (e.g., servers, databases) are dedicated to a single customer or tenant.

Implementation:

- In a single-tenancy model, each tenant has their own dedicated resources that are not shared with other tenants. This means that the software, databases, and infrastructure are isolated for each customer.
- **Example**: A company using a private cloud where the infrastructure and applications are solely for their use, ensuring that no other organization shares the same resources.
- **Advantages**: Greater control over data and security, higher customization, and isolation from other tenants, reducing the risk of "noisy neighbor" effects where one tenant's usage impacts another's performance.
- **Disadvantages**: Higher costs due to the need for dedicated resources and infrastructure for each tenant, and potentially lower resource utilization efficiency.

1. Multi-Tenancy:

Definition: Multi-tenancy is a cloud architecture model where a single instance of a software application and its associated resources are shared among multiple customers or tenants, with each tenant's data and configurations logically separated.

Implementation:

- In a multi-tenancy model, multiple tenants share the same infrastructure and software application while their data remains isolated and secure from one another. The cloud service provider ensures that each tenant's data is kept separate and secure, even though they share the same resources.
- **Example**: SaaS (Software as a Service) platforms like Salesforce or Office 365, where multiple customers use the same application but have individualized experiences, configurations, and data separation.
- **Advantages**: Cost-efficiency due to shared resources, easier maintenance and upgrades (as they are applied universally across all tenants), and better resource utilization.
- **Disadvantages**: Potential security concerns due to shared infrastructure, and less flexibility in customization compared to single-tenancy models.

Both models are used depending on the specific needs, security requirements, and budget constraints of the organization.

(c) What is Internet of Things (IOT)? What are the characteristics? Also explain industrial IoT, infrastructure IoT and internet of military things (IoMT) categories of IoT. 10

Ans: The Internet of Things (IoT) refers to the network of physical devices, vehicles, appliances, and other objects embedded with sensors, software, and other technologies that enable them to connect and exchange data over the internet. IoT allows these devices to collect and share data with each other, often autonomously, to achieve various goals such as improving efficiency, reducing costs, and enhancing user experience. IoT applications are widespread, ranging from smart homes and wearable devices to connected cars and industrial automation.

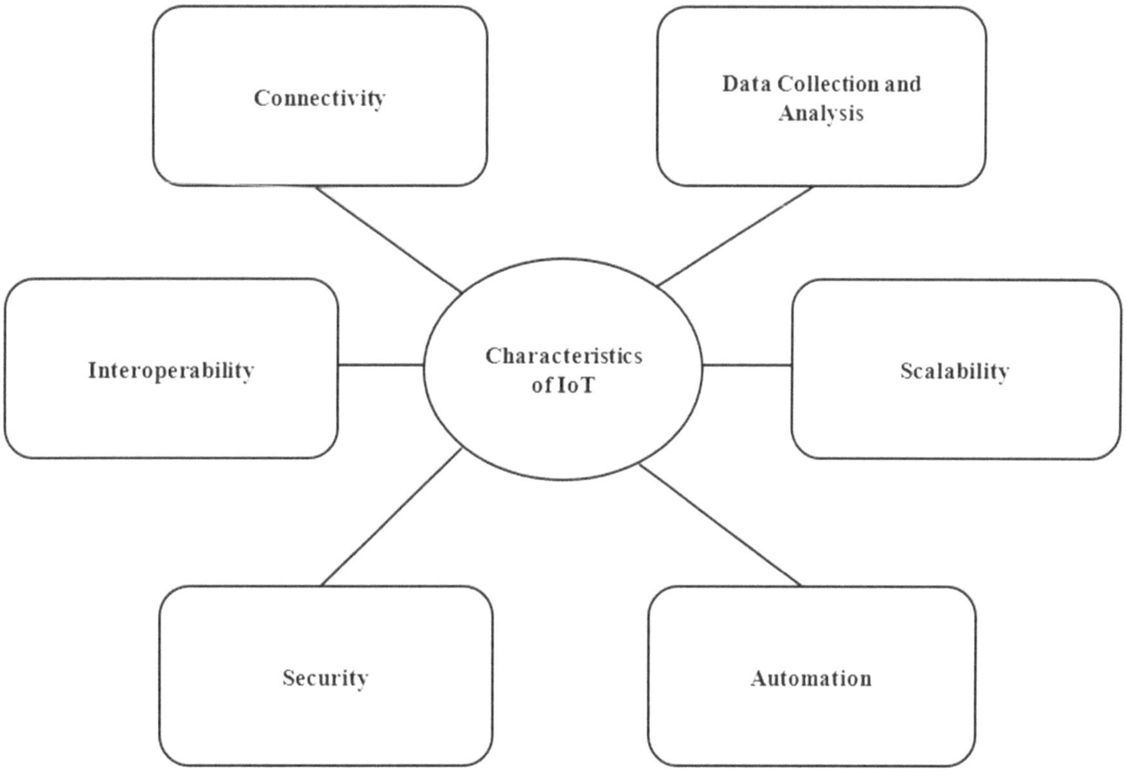

Characteristics of IoT:

1. Connectivity:

IoT devices are interconnected via various communication protocols such as Wi-Fi, Bluetooth, and cellular networks, enabling them to communicate with each other and with centralized systems or cloud platforms.

2. Data Collection and Analysis:
IoT devices continuously collect data from their environment through sensors and transmit this data for analysis. This data can be used to derive insights, make decisions, and trigger automated actions.
3. Interoperability:
IoT devices often come from different manufacturers and use different technologies. Interoperability refers to the ability of these devices to work together seamlessly despite these differences.
4. Scalability:
IoT systems can scale up to include thousands or even millions of devices, making them suitable for large-scale deployments in smart cities, industrial settings, and other environments.
5. Security:
As IoT devices are connected to the internet and often collect sensitive data, robust security measures are essential to protect the devices and the data they transmit from unauthorized access and cyber threats.
6. Automation:
IoT enables automation of processes through real-time data monitoring and control. Devices can operate independently or be controlled remotely without human intervention.

s

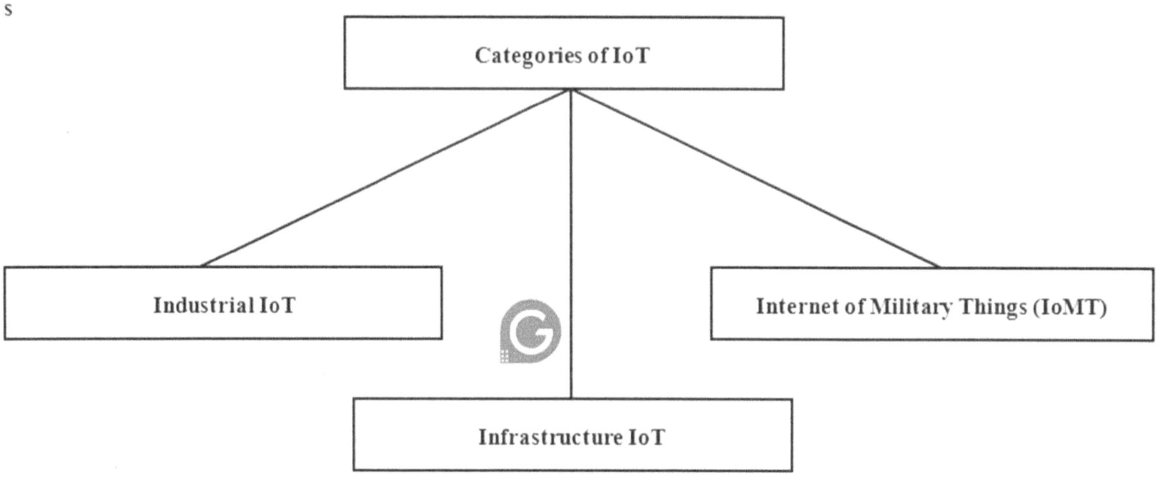

Categories of IoT
1. Industrial IoT:
Definition: Industrial IoT refers to the application of IoT technologies in industrial settings, such as manufacturing, energy, logistics, and agriculture, to enhance operational efficiency, productivity, and safety.
Explanation:
i. IoT involves the use of connected sensors, actuators, and devices to monitor and control industrial processes in real-time. For example, in manufacturing, IIoT can optimize production lines by collecting data on equipment performance and predicting maintenance needs before failures occur.
Applications: Predictive maintenance, remote monitoring, supply chain optimization, smart grids, and industrial automation.
2. Infrastructure IoT:
Definition: Infrastructure IoT refers to the integration of IoT technologies into large-scale infrastructure projects to enhance monitoring, maintenance, and management of critical systems such as transportation, utilities, and urban planning.
Explanation:
Infrastructure IoT enables the monitoring and management of infrastructure assets like bridges, roads, pipelines, and water systems through connected sensors and data analytics. For example, sensors embedded in a bridge can monitor structural integrity and provide early warnings of potential issues.
Applications: Smart cities, intelligent transportation systems, smart grids, and environmental monitoring.
3. Internet of Military Things (IoMT):
Definition: The Internet of Military Things (IoMT) refers to the use of IoT technologies in military operations and defence systems to enhance situational awareness, decision-making, and operational efficiency.

Explanation:
IoMT involves connecting various military assets such as vehicles, drones, weapons systems, and soldiers through a network to gather and share real-time data. This data can improve battlefield awareness, enable coordinated operations, and automate responses to threats.
Applications: Autonomous vehicles, battlefield surveillance, smart weapons, soldier health monitoring, and logistics management.

(d) Explain the differences between Fog computing and Edge computing. Draw the block diagram of 3-layer architecture of fog computing and explain all its layers. 10
Ans: Here is the comparison between Fog Computing and Edge Computing in tabular form, followed by the 3-layer architecture of Fog Computing:

Comparison Between Fog Computing and Edge Computing:

Aspect	Fog Computing	Edge Computing
Location of Processing	Intermediate layer between the edge and the cloud	Directly at the source or near the data-generating devices
Latency	Lower latency than cloud computing but higher than edge	Lowest latency as processing occurs at or near the data source
Scalability	More scalable, suitable for large-scale distributed networks	Less scalable for large-scale data aggregation
Data Processing	Processes data at fog nodes; aggregates and filters data	Processes data directly at edge devices; focuses on real-time actions
Architecture	Multi-layered (Edge → Fog → Cloud)	Primarily edge-focused; may bypass the cloud

3-Layer Architecture of Fog Computing:

Layer	Components	Functions
Edge Layer	IoT devices, sensors, actuators	- Data generation and collection - Initial data processing - Communication with fog nodes
Fog Layer	Fog nodes (routers, gateways, local servers)	- Data aggregation - Local processing and analytics - Real-time decision-making
Cloud Layer	Centralized cloud data centers	- Advanced data processing - Long-term storage - Integration with cloud services

This table format provides a concise comparison of Fog and Edge computing, along with an explanation of the 3-layer architecture of Fog Computing.

2. (a) Differentiate between cluster, grid and cloud computing with respect to its characteristics, physical structure, hardware, resources, applications, networking and scalability features. 10
Ans: Here's a differentiation between Cluster Computing, Grid Computing, and Cloud Computing based on various aspects:

Comparison Between Cluster, Grid, and Cloud Computing

Aspect	Cluster Computing	Grid Computing	Cloud Computing
Characteristics	- Homogeneous systems - Tight coupling - Single administrative domain	- Heterogeneous systems - Loose coupling - Multiple administrative domains	- Highly abstracted - On-demand service - Broad network access
Physical Structure	- Group of similar, tightly connected computers (nodes)	- Distributed across multiple locations, connected over a network	- Centralized or distributed infrastructure managed by cloud providers
Hardware	- Similar or identical hardware - Typically high-performance systems	- Varied hardware types - Can include commodity hardware and specialized systems	- Virtualized resources - Hosted on large-scale data centers with varied hardware
Resources	- Resources are dedicated and shared among nodes in a single cluster	- Resources are shared across different administrative domains - Resources are often scattered geographically	- On-demand resource allocation - Resources are pooled and can be scaled dynamically
Applications	- High-performance computing - Scientific simulations - Data-intensive tasks	- Complex computational tasks requiring distributed processing - Scientific research, large-scale simulations	- Web services - Big data processing - Enterprise applications, SaaS, PaaS, IaaS
Networking	- High-speed local area network (LAN) - Low latency communication between nodes	- Wide area network (WAN) - May involve public or private networks - Higher latency	- Internet-based networking - High-speed, scalable, with broader geographical reach
Scalability	- Limited scalability - Scaling usually involves adding more nodes to the cluster	- High scalability - Can expand by adding more resources from different locations	- Extremely high scalability - Elastic scaling with resources provisioned on-demand
Management	- Managed by a single organization - Centralized control	- Managed by multiple organizations - Decentralized control	- Managed by cloud providers - Automated and centralized management
Cost	- Fixed cost based on hardware and maintenance	- Lower cost due to sharing resources across multiple organizations	- Pay-as-you-go pricing model based on usage

Explanation:

1. Cluster Computing:

i. Characteristics: Involves a group of similar, closely located computers working together to perform computing tasks. It operates within a single administrative domain and typically uses similar hardware.

ii. Applications: Used in scenarios where high availability, load balancing, and parallel processing are required.

iii. Scalability: Scalability is limited to the number of nodes that can be added to the cluster, which are typically located in the same data center.

2. Grid Computing:

i. Characteristics: Distributed computing model where resources from different administrative domains are used collectively to perform large-scale computations. The systems involved are usually heterogeneous.

ii. Applications: Ideal for complex computational problems like large-scale simulations, scientific research, and tasks that require significant processing power spread across multiple locations.

iii. Scalability: Offers high scalability as resources can be added from different locations, often on an as-needed basis.

3. Cloud Computing:
i. Characteristics: Provides on-demand access to a shared pool of configurable computing resources such as networks, servers, storage, applications, and services. It abstracts the physical infrastructure from the user, offering scalability and flexibility.
ii. Applications: Widely used for a range of applications including web hosting, big data analytics, disaster recovery, and deployment of virtualized environments.
iii. Scalability: Highly scalable, allowing resources to be quickly scaled up or down based on demand, often automatically.
This table and explanations provide a clear distinction between the three computing models in terms of their structure, resources, applications, and scalability.

(b) What is Auto scaling in cloud? Write and explain fixed amount auto scaling algorithm. 10
Ans: Auto scaling in cloud computing refers to the process of automatically adjusting the number of active computational resources, such as virtual machines or containers, in response to the current demand. This means scaling out (adding more resources) when demand increases and scaling in (removing resources) when demand decreases. The primary goal of auto scaling is to ensure that applications maintain optimal performance and availability while minimizing costs by only using the necessary resources.

Fixed Amount Auto Scaling Algorithm
The Fixed Amount Auto Scaling Algorithm is a straightforward approach to auto scaling where a predefined, fixed number of resources (e.g., virtual machines, instances) are added or removed based on certain threshold conditions, such as CPU utilization, memory usage, or request rate.

Steps and Explanation of the Fixed Amount Auto Scaling Algorithm:
1. Define Thresholds:
Upper Threshold: Set a maximum threshold for resource utilization, such as CPU usage reaching 80%.
Lower Threshold: Set a minimum threshold for resource utilization, such as CPU usage dropping below 30%.

2. Monitor Resource Utilization:
Continuously monitor the resource usage metrics (e.g., CPU, memory, network bandwidth) of the application or service.

3. Check Against Thresholds:
Compare the current resource utilization with the defined thresholds.

4. Scale Out (Add Resources):
Condition: If the resource utilization exceeds the upper threshold (e.g., CPU usage > 80%).
Action: Add a fixed number of resources (e.g., 2 more virtual machines) to handle the increased load. This helps in distributing the load more evenly and maintaining performance.

5. Scale In (Remove Resources):
Condition: If the resource utilization drops below the lower threshold (e.g., CPU usage < 30%).
Action: Remove a fixed number of resources (e.g., 2 virtual machines) to avoid over-provisioning and reduce costs.

6. Wait Time:
Introduce a wait or cool-down period after scaling actions to allow the system to stabilize before the next scaling action is considered. This prevents rapid fluctuations in scaling decisions.

7. Repeat Monitoring:
Continue monitoring resource utilization and repeat the process based on the current demand.

Example Scenario:
Imagine a web application running on cloud infrastructure:
- **Upper Threshold**: CPU usage > 80%
- **Lower Threshold**: CPU usage < 30%

- **Fixed Scaling Amount**: Add or remove 2 virtual machines
- **Initial State**: The application runs with 4 virtual machines.
- **Increased Load**: Traffic increases, and CPU usage across the instances averages 85%.
    i. **Action**: The algorithm triggers scaling out, adding 2 more virtual machines, bringing the total to 6.
- **Decreased Load**: Traffic decreases, and CPU usage drops to 25%.
    i. **Action**: The algorithm triggers scaling in, removing 2 virtual machines, reducing the total to 4.

Benefits of Fixed Amount Auto Scaling:
- **Simplicity**: Easy to implement and understand.
- **Predictability**: Resource scaling is predictable due to the fixed increment/decrement.
- **Cost Control**: Helps prevent over-provisioning of resources, leading to cost savings.

Limitations:
i. **Lack of Flexibility**: The fixed amount may not always be ideal for all situations, especially if demand changes are significant.
ii. **Potential for Over/Under Scaling**: If the fixed amount is too large or too small relative to demand fluctuations, it could lead to over-scaling (wasting resources) or under-scaling (performance degradation).
The Fixed Amount Auto Scaling Algorithm is suitable for scenarios where resource demand patterns are relatively predictable, and the system can tolerate slight over or under-provisioning.

3. (a) Define resource pooling in cloud environment. In this context, explain the following: 10
(i) Server Pools
(ii) Storage Pools
(iii) Network Pools
Ans: Definition of Resource Pooling in Cloud Environment:
Resource Pooling in a cloud environment refers to the cloud provider's ability to serve multiple customers (tenants) by dynamically allocating and reallocating resources such as computing power, storage, and network bandwidth from a shared pool. This means that the physical and virtual resources are pooled together and can be assigned or reassigned according to the demand, ensuring efficient utilization of resources. Resource pooling enables multi-tenancy, where multiple users share the same physical infrastructure while keeping their data and applications isolated.

(i) Server Pools:
Server Pools refer to a collection of physical or virtual servers grouped together to provide computing resources on-demand to multiple users or applications. In a cloud environment, server pools allow cloud providers to allocate and manage computational resources dynamically based on the needs of the users.
Functionality:
Server pools provide the computational power necessary for running applications, processing data, and executing tasks.
These resources can be scaled up or down automatically based on the demand, ensuring that the right amount of computing power is always available without over-provisioning.
Benefits:
Scalability: Easily add or remove servers from the pool to meet demand.
Load Balancing: Distribute workloads evenly across the servers to prevent any single server from being overwhelmed.
Redundancy: In case of server failure, the workload can be shifted to another server in the pool, ensuring high availability.

(ii) Storage Pools:
Storage Pools refer to a collection of storage resources (such as hard drives, SSDs, or other storage devices) aggregated to form a centralized storage resource that can be allocated to various users or applications as needed.
Functionality:
Storage pools allow cloud providers to offer scalable and flexible storage solutions to users. The storage resources are managed centrally, and users can be allocated specific amounts of storage based on their requirements.
Storage pools can consist of various types of storage, such as block storage, object storage, or file storage, depending on the needs of the application or user.

Benefits:
Elasticity: Easily expand or contract storage space as needed, allowing for flexible storage management.
Data Redundancy and Backup: Storage pools often incorporate redundancy and backup mechanisms, ensuring data integrity and availability even in the event of hardware failures.
Cost Efficiency: By pooling storage resources, providers can optimize the use of storage hardware, reducing costs for both the provider and the user.

(iii) Network Pools:
Network Pools refer to the aggregation of networking resources such as bandwidth, IP addresses, and virtual network interfaces that can be dynamically allocated to various users or applications in the cloud environment.
Functionality:
Network pools enable cloud providers to manage and allocate network resources effectively. These resources can include virtual networks, subnets, and network bandwidth.
The network resources in a pool are typically virtualized, allowing for the creation of virtual private networks (VPNs), virtual LANs (VLANs), and other network configurations tailored to user needs.
Benefits:
Flexibility: Network pools allow for the quick and easy creation of complex network topologies without the need for physical hardware changes.
Security: By isolating network traffic within virtual networks, cloud providers can offer secure communication channels for users.
Efficiency: Network resources can be allocated based on demand, ensuring optimal use of available bandwidth and minimizing bottlenecks.

(b) With the help of a block diagram, explain the 4-levels in a cloud architecture. 10
Ans: Cloud architecture typically consists of multiple layers that work together to provide comprehensive cloud services. The most common model is the 4-level architecture, which includes the following layers:
1. Infrastructure Layer (Hardware Layer)
2. Platform Layer
3. Application Layer
4. User Layer (Client Layer)

Block Diagram of 4-Level Cloud Architecture:
Here's how you can visualize the 4-level cloud architecture in a block diagram:

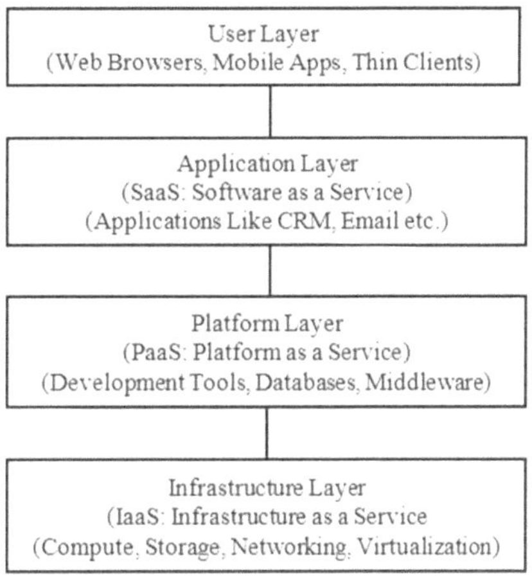

Explanation of Each Layer:
1. Infrastructure Layer (IaaS - Infrastructure as a Service):
Description: This is the foundational layer of cloud architecture. It provides the basic computing infrastructure such as servers, storage, networking, and virtualization. It allows users to rent virtual machines, storage, and other fundamental computing resources over the internet.
Components: Physical and virtual servers, storage devices, networking components, and virtualization technologies.
Function: Enables the creation of virtualized environments where users can deploy and manage their own applications and data.

2. Platform Layer (PaaS - Platform as a Service):
Description: This layer provides a platform that allows developers to build, test, and deploy applications without worrying about the underlying infrastructure. It abstracts the complexity of managing the hardware and operating systems.
Components: Application development frameworks, databases, middleware, runtime environments, and API management tools.
Function: Offers a development environment where users can create applications using pre-built tools and components. It simplifies the development process and accelerates time-to-market.

3. Application Layer (SaaS - Software as a Service):
Description: This layer provides software applications that are hosted and managed by the cloud provider and are available to users over the internet. Users can access these applications via web browsers or thin clients without installing or managing the software themselves.
Components: End-user applications such as CRM systems, email services, office productivity tools, and collaboration platforms.
Function: Delivers software applications as a service, eliminating the need for users to manage the underlying infrastructure or platforms.

4. User Layer (Client Layer):
Description: This is the topmost layer where end-users interact with the cloud services. It includes the interfaces and devices that users utilize to access cloud services, such as web browsers, mobile apps, and other client devices.
Components: Web browsers, mobile apps, thin clients, and APIs that connect to the cloud services.
Function: Provides the interface through which users interact with cloud services. It ensures a seamless user experience across different devices and platforms.

4. (a) Define virtualization. Explain its underlying abstraction. Also mention the features provided by virtualization environment. 10

Ans: Virtualization is a technology that allows the creation of multiple simulated environments or dedicated resources from a single physical hardware system. It involves creating a virtual version of something, such as an operating system, a server, a storage device, or network resources, so that multiple systems can share the underlying hardware resources more efficiently.

Underlying Abstraction:
The underlying abstraction in virtualization is the decoupling of physical hardware from the software that runs on it. This abstraction layer is typically provided by a hypervisor (or virtual machine monitor), which is software that sits between the physical hardware and the operating system. The hypervisor creates and manages virtual machines (VMs), allowing multiple operating systems and applications to run simultaneously on a single physical machine.
The abstraction occurs because the hypervisor presents virtual hardware to the guest operating systems, making them believe they are running on dedicated hardware. The actual physical resources, such as CPU, memory, and storage, are shared among the virtual machines in a way that is transparent to the VMs.

Features Provided by a Virtualization Environment Isolation: Virtual machines are isolated from each other, meaning that processes running in one VM do not affect those in another VM. This isolation also extends to security, preventing VMs from accessing each other's data.
- **Resource Allocation:** Virtualization allows for dynamic allocation of physical resources like CPU, memory, and storage to different VMs based on demand, improving resource utilization.
- **Flexibility and Scalability:** Virtualization makes it easy to deploy, manage, and scale computing environments. New virtual machines can be created quickly, and existing VMs can be scaled up or down as needed.
- **Cost Efficiency:** By running multiple virtual machines on a single physical server, organizations can reduce the number of physical servers needed, leading to cost savings on hardware, power, cooling, and maintenance.
- **Improved Disaster Recovery:** Virtual machines can be easily backed up, replicated, and restored, providing enhanced disaster recovery options compared to physical systems.
- **Live Migration:** Virtualization environments often support the live migration of virtual machines from one physical host to another without downtime, enabling maintenance and load balancing without interrupting services.

- **Centralized Management:** Virtualization platforms often include management tools that allow administrators to manage and monitor multiple virtual machines from a single interface, simplifying system administration.
- **Enhanced Testing and Development:** Virtualization provides an ideal environment for testing and development by allowing developers to create multiple environments with different configurations on a single physical machine.

Virtualization abstracts physical resources, allowing multiple virtual systems to operate independently on a single physical system. This leads to increased flexibility, resource efficiency, and better management of IT environments.

(b) Explain the following communication protocols with reference to the IoT devices: 10
(i) IPv6
(ii) MQTT
(iii) CoAP
(iv) XMPP

(i) IPv6

IPv6 (Internet Protocol version 6) is the most recent version of the Internet Protocol (IP), designed to address the limitations of IPv4, particularly the exhaustion of IP addresses. It provides a vastly larger address space, allowing for an almost unlimited number of unique IP addresses, which is crucial for the scalability of IoT (Internet of Things) devices.

Role in IoT:

- **Address Space:** IoT involves connecting a massive number of devices to the internet. IPv6's large address space (128-bit addressing) ensures that each IoT device can have a unique IP address, enabling seamless connectivity.
- **Auto-configuration:** IPv6 supports features like stateless address autoconfiguration (SLAAC), which allows IoT devices to automatically generate their own IP addresses, simplifying network management.
- **Efficient Routing:** IPv6 improves routing efficiency and the hierarchical structure of the address allocation, reducing the size of routing tables, which is beneficial for IoT networks with large numbers of devices.
- **Security:** IPv6 was designed with security in mind, incorporating IPsec (Internet Protocol Security) for end-to-end encryption and secure data transmission, which is essential for the security of IoT devices.

(ii) MQTT (Message Queuing Telemetry Transport)

MQTT is a lightweight messaging protocol designed for low-bandwidth, high-latency, or unreliable networks, making it ideal for IoT applications. It follows the publish-subscribe model, where devices (clients) communicate through a broker.

Role in IoT:

- **Low Power Consumption:** MQTT's lightweight nature makes it suitable for IoT devices that have limited processing power and memory, such as sensors and actuators.
- **Publish-Subscribe Model:** The publish-subscribe model allows for efficient and flexible communication. Devices can publish data to a broker without knowing the subscribers, and subscribers can receive data without knowing the publishers, making the system scalable.
- **QoS (Quality of Service):** MQTT provides different levels of QoS, ensuring reliable message delivery, which is crucial for IoT applications where data loss could be critical.

Minimal Bandwidth Usage: MQTT's design minimizes the use of bandwidth, making it ideal for IoT devices operating in environments with constrained network resources.

(iii) CoAP (Constrained Application Protocol)

CoAP is a web transfer protocol designed for constrained devices and networks, which are common in IoT environments. It is based on the REST model, similar to HTTP, but optimized for low-power, low-bandwidth networks.

Role in IoT:

- **Lightweight Protocol:** CoAP is specifically designed for devices with limited processing capabilities and memory, which are typical in IoT.
- **Efficient Resource Utilization:** CoAP uses the UDP protocol, which is less resource-intensive than TCP, making it suitable for IoT devices that operate in resource-constrained environments.
- **Interoperability:** CoAP allows IoT devices to communicate over the internet, leveraging the REST architecture, which is widely used and understood in web services.

- **Support for Multicast:** CoAP supports multicast, allowing efficient communication between multiple devices, which is useful in scenarios like sensor networks where data needs to be shared among many devices.
- **Security:** CoAP supports DTLS (Datagram Transport Layer Security) for secure communication, which is essential for IoT devices that exchange sensitive data.

(iv) XMPP (Extensible Messaging and Presence Protocol)
XMPP is a communication protocol that was originally designed for instant messaging but has been adapted for use in IoT. It is an XML-based protocol that provides real-time communication.
Role in IoT:
- **Real-time Communication:** XMPP's real-time communication capabilities are beneficial for IoT devices that need to exchange information instantly, such as in smart home systems or industrial automation.
- **Decentralization:** XMPP is a decentralized protocol, meaning there is no central server, which makes it resilient and scalable, suitable for IoT networks where devices are distributed across different locations.
- **Security:** XMPP supports encryption and authentication mechanisms, ensuring secure communication between IoT devices.
- **Extensibility:** XMPP's flexible and extensible nature allows it to be customized for various IoT use cases, supporting a wide range of applications from simple messaging to complex data exchange.
- **Presence Information:** XMPP's presence feature allows IoT devices to announce their status to the network, which can be used to manage device availability and connectivity.

These protocols, IPv6, MQTT, CoAP, and XMPP,each play a crucial role in enabling communication among IoT devices, addressing different needs such as addressing, message delivery, resource constraints, and real-time communication.

5. Write short notes on the following: 5*4 = 20
(a) Multihoming and its types
(b) Horizontal scaling in cloud environment
(c) Challenges in cloud computing
(d) Applications of edge computing
Ans: (a) Multihoming and Its Types
Multihoming refers to a network configuration in which a device, server, or network is connected to more than one internet service provider (ISP) or network. This setup enhances reliability, availability, and redundancy, ensuring continuous connectivity even if one connection fails.

Types of Multihoming:
1. Single-homed: A basic setup where a single device or network is connected to a single ISP, but with multiple IP addresses or network interfaces. This is the simplest form of multihoming but lacks true redundancy.
2. Dual-homed: In this setup, a device or network connects to two different ISPs. It provides better redundancy and reliability because if one ISP fails, the other can maintain the connection.
3. Multi-homed: Here, a device or network is connected to more than two ISPs. This setup provides the highest level of redundancy, load balancing, and failover capabilities, making it ideal for critical systems that require constant uptime.
4. Host Multihoming: A specific type where an individual host (such as a server) is connected to multiple networks or ISPs, often used for load balancing and fault tolerance.

(b) Horizontal Scaling in Cloud Environment
Horizontal Scaling, also known as "scaling out," refers to the process of adding more machines or instances to a cloud environment to handle increased load or demand. Instead of upgrading the power or capacity of existing machines (vertical scaling), horizontal scaling involves deploying additional instances of servers, databases, or other resources to distribute the workload.

Benefits of Horizontal Scaling:
- **Improved Performance:** By distributing the load across multiple instances, horizontal scaling can improve performance and reduce latency.
- **High Availability:** Adding more instances enhances redundancy, reducing the risk of downtime if one instance fails.

- **Cost-Effectiveness:** Horizontal scaling can be more cost-effective in cloud environments, where resources can be easily added or removed based on demand.
- **Flexibility:** It allows organizations to dynamically scale resources up or down based on real-time demand, optimizing resource utilization.

(c) Challenges in Cloud Computing

Cloud computing offers numerous benefits, but it also presents several challenges that organizations must address:

1. **Security and Privacy:** Storing sensitive data on third-party servers raises concerns about data breaches, unauthorized access, and compliance with data protection regulations.
2. **Data Transfer and Bandwidth:** Moving large amounts of data to and from the cloud can be time-consuming and costly, especially in regions with limited bandwidth.
3. **Vendor Lock-In:** Once an organization commits to a particular cloud provider, migrating to another provider can be difficult and costly due to differences in platforms, tools, and APIs.
4. **Downtime and Reliability:** Although cloud providers offer high availability, outages and downtime can still occur, impacting business operations.
5. **Cost Management:** While cloud computing can reduce infrastructure costs, managing and predicting costs can be challenging, particularly with variable usage patterns.
6. **Compliance and Legal Issues:** Ensuring compliance with industry regulations (e.g., GDPR, HIPAA) and understanding the legal implications of data storage across different jurisdictions can be complex.

(d) Applications of Edge Computing

Edge Computing is a distributed computing paradigm that brings computation and data storage closer to the location where it is needed, reducing latency and bandwidth usage. It is particularly useful in scenarios where real-time processing is critical.

Applications of Edge Computing:

1. **Autonomous Vehicles:** Edge computing enables real-time data processing from sensors and cameras in autonomous vehicles, allowing for immediate decision-making without relying on remote cloud servers.
2. **Smart Cities:** Edge computing supports smart city applications like traffic management, surveillance, and environmental monitoring by processing data locally and reducing the load on central servers.
3. **IoT Devices:** Many IoT devices rely on edge computing to process data locally, reducing the need to send large volumes of data to the cloud, thus saving bandwidth and improving response times.
4. **Healthcare:** In healthcare, edge computing is used for real-time monitoring and analysis of patient data from medical devices, enabling faster diagnosis and treatment.
5. **Industrial Automation:** In manufacturing and industrial environments, edge computing facilitates real-time processing and control of machinery, leading to improved efficiency and reduced downtime.
6. **Content Delivery:** Edge computing is used in content delivery networks (CDNs) to cache and deliver content closer to the user, improving load times and reducing latency for streaming services and websites.

These notes provide an overview of each concept, highlighting their importance and applications in modern technology environments.

MCS – 227

Master Of Computer Applications (MCA)
Chapter 2: Term-End Examination, Dec, 2022
MCS-227: CLOUD COMPUTING AND Iot

Time: 3 Hours
Maximum Marks: 100
Weightage: 70
Note: Question No. 1 is compulsory. Answer any three Questions from the rest.

1. (a) What is resource provisioning in cloud computing? Explain the static and dynamic approaches of resource provisioning. Mention their advantages and disadvantages. 10

Ans: Resource Provisioning in cloud computing refers to the process of allocating and managing computational resources (such as CPU, memory, storage, and network bandwidth) to applications or services in a cloud environment. The goal is to ensure that applications have the necessary resources to function efficiently and meet performance requirements while optimizing resource utilization and costs.

Static and Dynamic Approaches of Resource Provisioning
Static Resource Provisioning:
In static resource provisioning, resources are allocated based on predefined requirements or estimates that do not change dynamically. The resources are provisioned for a specific workload or application in advance, often based on peak usage predictions. This approach is typically used when the workload is predictable and does not vary significantly over time.

Advantages:
- **Simplicity:** Static provisioning is straightforward to implement and manage since resources are allocated based on fixed requirements.
- **Predictability:** Because resources are provisioned based on known requirements, there is little variability in resource availability, making it easier to ensure consistent performance.
- **Cost Predictability:** Fixed resources mean costs are easier to predict and manage, as the resource usage does not fluctuate.

Disadvantages:
- **Resource Underutilization:** If the allocated resources exceed the actual demand, it can lead to underutilization and wasted resources, increasing costs unnecessarily.
- **Inflexibility:** Static provisioning lacks the flexibility to handle unexpected spikes in demand, potentially leading to performance issues or service degradation.
- **Scalability Issues:** In environments with fluctuating workloads, static provisioning may not scale effectively, requiring manual adjustments or over-provisioning to handle peak loads.

Dynamic Resource Provisioning:
Dynamic resource provisioning, also known as elastic provisioning, involves the automatic allocation and deallocation of resources based on real-time demand. Resources are adjusted dynamically to match the current workload, allowing for more efficient use of cloud resources. This approach leverages cloud features like autoscaling to adapt to changing requirements.

Advantages:
- **Optimal Resource Utilization:** Resources are allocated based on actual demand, reducing waste and ensuring that resources are used efficiently.
- **Scalability:** Dynamic provisioning allows for seamless scaling up or down in response to workload changes, ensuring that applications can handle varying loads without manual intervention.
- **Cost Efficiency:** By only using the resources that are needed, dynamic provisioning can lead to significant cost savings compared to static provisioning.

- **Improved Performance:** Applications can maintain performance levels even during unexpected demand spikes because resources are provisioned in real-time.

Disadvantages:
- **Complexity:** Dynamic provisioning is more complex to implement and manage, requiring sophisticated monitoring, automation, and orchestration tools.
- **Latency:** There may be a slight delay in resource allocation as the system adjusts to changing demands, which can affect performance if not managed correctly.
- **Cost Unpredictability:** While dynamic provisioning can reduce costs, the variability in resource usage can make it difficult to predict overall expenses, especially in highly variable workloads.

Both approaches have their specific use cases, and the choice between them depends on the nature of the application, workload variability, and organizational priorities regarding cost, performance, and management complexity.

(b) Define Load Balancing. Explain the following algorithms with reference to load balancing: 10
(i) Static algorithm approach
(ii) Weighted Round Robin

Ans: Load Balancing is a technique used in distributed computing and cloud environments to distribute workloads evenly across multiple servers or resources. The primary goal of load balancing is to ensure that no single server or resource is overwhelmed by too much work, which could lead to performance degradation or failure. Load balancing helps to optimize resource use, maximize throughput, minimize response time, and avoid overload of any single resource.

Load Balancing Algorithms

(i) Static Algorithm Approach

In the static algorithm approach, load balancing decisions are made based on predefined criteria and do not change dynamically in response to the current system state. The static algorithms allocate the load to servers or resources at the start of the process and do not adjust the allocation based on changes in workload or system performance.

Examples of Static Algorithms:
Round Robin: In this algorithm, requests are distributed evenly across all available servers in a circular order. Each server gets the next request in line, regardless of the server's current load or performance.
Random Allocation: In this approach, incoming requests are assigned to servers randomly without considering their current load or capacity.

Advantages:
- **Simplicity:** Static algorithms are easy to implement and understand, requiring minimal computational overhead.
- **Predictability:** Since the load distribution is predetermined, the behavior of the system is predictable, making it easier to manage.

Disadvantages:
- **Inefficiency:** Static algorithms do not account for variations in server load, leading to potential underutilization or overloading of some servers.
- **Lack of Adaptability:** These algorithms cannot adapt to changes in workload or system state, which may result in suboptimal performance in dynamic environments.

(ii) Weighted Round Robin

Weighted Round Robin (WRR) is an extension of the Round Robin algorithm, where each server or resource is assigned a weight based on its capacity or capability. Requests are distributed to the servers based on their weight, meaning servers with higher weights receive more requests than those with lower weights.

How It Works:
- Each server is assigned a weight, which typically corresponds to its processing power, memory, or other resources.
- The load balancer distributes incoming requests in a round-robin fashion, but servers with higher weights receive more requests in proportion to their weight.

- For example, if Server A has a weight of 3 and Server B has a weight of 1, Server A will receive three requests for every one request sent to Server B.

Advantages:
- **Resource Utilization:** WRR takes into account the capacity of each server, ensuring that more powerful servers handle a proportionally larger share of the workload.
- **Flexibility:** It allows for customized load distribution based on server capabilities, leading to better overall system performance.

Disadvantages:
- **Static Nature:** While WRR improves upon basic Round Robin by considering server weights, it still operates based on predefined weights and does not dynamically adjust to real-time load changes.
- **Complex Configuration:** Determining the appropriate weights for each server can be complex, especially in environments where server performance characteristics change over time.

(c) Discuss the following baseline technologies of IoT: 10

(i) Security in IoT
(ii) IoT Analytics
(iii) IoT Processors
(iv) IoT Standards and Ecosystems

Ans: (i) Security in IoT

Security in the Internet of Things (IoT) is a critical aspect that involves protecting IoT devices, networks, and data from unauthorized access, attacks, and breaches. Given the vast number of devices and their integration into everyday life, securing these devices is paramount to ensuring the safety and privacy of users.

Key Aspects of IoT Security:
- **Data Encryption:** Ensuring that data transmitted between IoT devices and the cloud or other devices is encrypted to prevent interception and unauthorized access.
- **Authentication and Authorization:** Implementing robust authentication mechanisms (e.g., multi-factor authentication) to verify the identity of devices and users. Authorization ensures that only approved devices or users can access specific data or perform certain actions.
- **Device Integrity:** Protecting IoT devices from being compromised through malware, ensuring that only authorized firmware or software updates are applied.
- **Network Security:** Securing the networks over which IoT devices communicate to prevent eavesdropping, man-in-the-middle attacks, and other network-based threats.
- **Security by Design:** Integrating security features into the design and development of IoT devices, rather than treating security as an afterthought.

Challenges:
- **Limited Resources:** Many IoT devices have limited processing power, memory, and storage, making it difficult to implement traditional security measures.
- **Scale:** The sheer number of IoT devices presents a challenge in managing and securing all endpoints.
- **Diverse Ecosystem:** The diversity of IoT devices, operating systems, and protocols can create interoperability issues, complicating security efforts.

(ii) IoT Analytics

IoT Analytics refers to the process of collecting, processing, and analysing data generated by IoT devices to derive actionable insights. IoT generates massive amounts of data, and analytics helps in making sense of this data to improve decision-making, enhance operations, and create new business opportunities.

Key Components of IoT Analytics:
- **Data Collection:** Gathering data from various IoT devices and sensors, which may include structured, semi-structured, or unstructured data.
- **Data Processing:** Using real-time processing frameworks to handle the continuous stream of data generated by IoT devices. This often involves edge computing to process data closer to the source.
- **Data Storage:** Storing large volumes of IoT data in databases or data lakes, ensuring that it is accessible for analysis.

- **Data Analysis:** Applying advanced analytical techniques, such as machine learning, artificial intelligence, and statistical methods, to extract insights from IoT data.
- **Visualization:** Presenting the analysed data in the form of dashboards, reports, or visualizations to help stakeholders understand the results and make informed decisions.

Applications:
- **Predictive Maintenance:** Analysing data from industrial IoT devices to predict equipment failures before they occur, reducing downtime and maintenance costs.
- **Smart Cities:** Using IoT analytics to optimize traffic flow, manage energy consumption, and improve public safety.
- **Healthcare:** Monitoring patient data in real-time to provide personalized treatment and early intervention in medical emergencies.

(iii) IoT Processors

IoT Processors are the central processing units (CPUs) or microcontrollers (MCUs) that power IoT devices, enabling them to perform computations, process data, and interact with other devices or networks. These processors are designed to meet the specific needs of IoT devices, such as low power consumption, real-time processing, and connectivity.

Types of IoT Processors:
- **Microcontrollers (MCUs):** Low-power processors with integrated memory and peripherals, commonly used in IoT devices for simple control tasks, data acquisition, and communication.
- **System-on-Chip (SoC):** Combines multiple components, such as CPU, memory, and communication modules, onto a single chip, providing a compact and efficient solution for IoT devices.
- **Application Processors:** More powerful processors used in complex IoT applications that require higher computational capabilities, such as video processing, AI inference, or machine learning at the edge.

Key Features:
- **Low Power Consumption:** IoT processors are optimized for energy efficiency, allowing devices to operate for extended periods on battery power.
- **Real-time Processing:** Some IoT processors are designed to handle real-time data processing, essential for applications like industrial automation or autonomous vehicles.
- **Connectivity:** IoT processors often include built-in communication modules (e.g., Wi-Fi, Bluetooth, Zigbee) to enable seamless connectivity with other devices and networks.

Challenges:
- **Balancing Power and Performance:** IoT processors need to provide adequate performance while minimizing power consumption, which can be challenging in resource-constrained environments.
- **Security:** Integrating security features directly into the processor is essential to protect IoT devices from cyber threats.

(iv) IoT Standards and Ecosystems

IoT Standards and Ecosystems refer to the set of protocols, frameworks, and guidelines that enable interoperability, security, and scalability within the IoT landscape. These standards ensure that IoT devices from different manufacturers can work together seamlessly and that the ecosystem supports a wide range of applications.

Key IoT Standards:
- **IEEE 802.15.4:** A standard for low-rate wireless personal area networks (LR-WPANs), commonly used in IoT devices for communication protocols like Zigbee.
- **MQTT (Message Queuing Telemetry Transport):** A lightweight messaging protocol widely used in IoT for reliable communication in low-bandwidth, high-latency environments.
- **CoAP (Constrained Application Protocol):** A web transfer protocol optimized for constrained devices and networks, similar to HTTP but more lightweight.
- **LWM2M (Lightweight Machine to Machine):** A protocol designed for managing IoT devices, providing features like device provisioning, monitoring, and firmware updates.

IoT Ecosystems: An IoT ecosystem comprises the interconnected network of devices, platforms, standards, and stakeholders that work together to deliver IoT services and solutions. Key components of an IoT ecosystem include:

- **IoT Devices:** The physical devices that collect and transmit data.
- **IoT Platforms:** Cloud-based platforms that provide the infrastructure and tools needed to manage IoT devices, process data, and develop applications.
- **Network Protocols:** The communication protocols that enable data exchange between devices, networks, and platforms.
- **Standards Organizations:** Bodies like the Internet Engineering Task Force (IETF) and the International Organization for Standardization (ISO) that develop and maintain IoT standards.

Challenges:
- **Interoperability:** Ensuring that devices from different manufacturers can communicate and work together, which requires adherence to common standards.
- **Fragmentation:** The IoT landscape is highly fragmented, with many competing standards and platforms, making it challenging to create a unified ecosystem.
- **Security:** Maintaining security across the entire IoT ecosystem is complex due to the large number of devices, networks, and platforms involved.

These baseline technologies form the foundation of the IoT landscape, enabling the development, deployment, and management of IoT devices and applications across various industries.

(d) Define Edge Computing. Draw a block diagram of Cloud-Fog-Edge collaboration and explain all its layers. 10

Edge Computing is a distributed computing paradigm that brings computation and data storage closer to the location where it is needed, such as IoT devices or local servers. Instead of sending data to a centralized cloud for processing, edge computing allows for data to be processed at the "edge" of the network, near the source of data generation. This approach reduces latency, conserves bandwidth, and enables real-time processing, which is crucial for applications like autonomous vehicles, smart cities, and industrial automation.

Block Diagram of Cloud-Fog-Edge Collaboration

Below is a conceptual explanation of the Cloud-Fog-Edge collaboration along with a description of its layers:

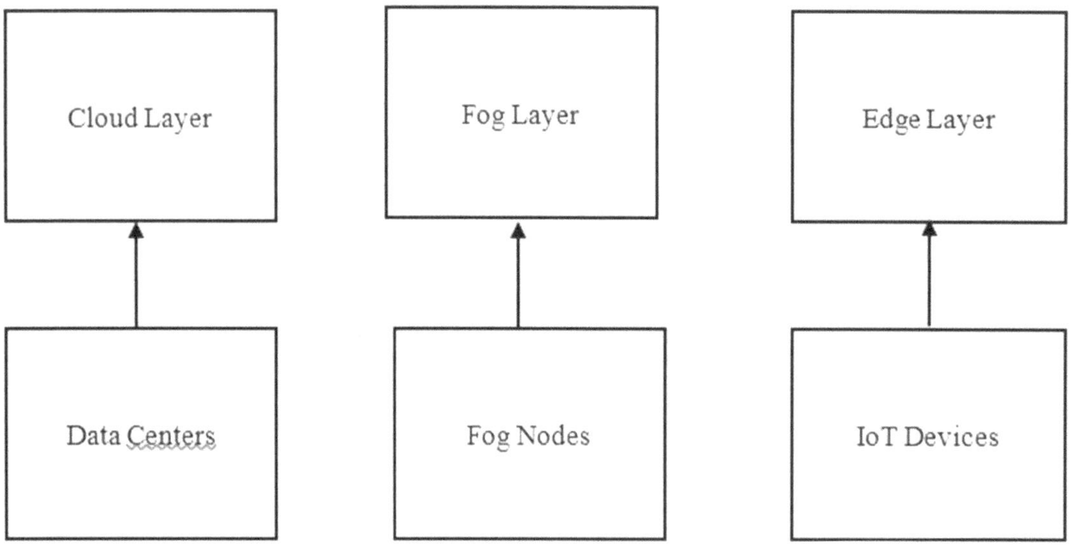

Explanation of Layers:

1. Cloud Layer:

Description:

The cloud layer represents centralized data centers and servers that provide large-scale storage, processing power, and advanced analytics capabilities. Cloud computing is responsible for handling complex computations, long-term data storage, and large-scale data processing.

Functions:
Data Storage: Massive data storage capabilities are provided, allowing for long-term storage and historical analysis.
Advanced Analytics: The cloud can perform complex machine learning, AI processing, and large-scale data analytics that require significant computational resources.
Global Access: Data and services stored in the cloud can be accessed from anywhere in the world, providing scalability and flexibility.

2. Fog Layer:
Description:
The fog layer acts as an intermediary between the cloud and edge layers. It consists of fog nodes, which are typically local servers, gateways, or other intermediary devices that process data closer to the source than the cloud but further away than the edge.
Functions:
Data Aggregation: Fog nodes collect and aggregate data from multiple edge devices, reducing the volume of data that needs to be sent to the cloud.
Intermediate Processing: Some data processing and analysis are performed at the fog layer, reducing latency and providing quicker responses compared to cloud processing.
Security: Fog nodes can provide additional layers of security by filtering and securing data before it is sent to the cloud.
3. Edge Layer:
Description:
The edge layer is where data is generated and initially processed, often on the IoT devices themselves. This layer is closest to the data source, and it is crucial for real-time data processing and decision-making.
Functions:
Real-Time Processing: Edge devices process data locally, allowing for real-time decision-making and reducing the need to send all data to the cloud.
Low Latency: By processing data at the source, edge computing significantly reduces latency, which is critical for applications like autonomous vehicles or industrial automation.
Bandwidth Efficiency: Edge computing reduces the amount of data that needs to be transmitted to the cloud, saving bandwidth and reducing costs.

Collaboration Between Layers:
1. Data Flow:
Data is initially generated and processed at the edge layer for immediate decision-making. Only necessary data is sent to the fog layer for further aggregation and intermediate processing. Finally, the cloud layer handles long-term storage, complex analysis, and large-scale data processing.
2. Scalability:
The collaboration between these layers allows for scalable, efficient, and secure processing of massive amounts of data generated by IoT devices. Each layer complements the other, providing a balance between real-time processing, resource efficiency, and computational power.
3. Use Cases:
Applications like smart cities, industrial IoT, and autonomous vehicles benefit from this collaboration, as it allows for real-time data processing at the edge while leveraging the computational power of the cloud for more complex tasks.

This collaboration of cloud, fog, and edge computing enables a flexible, efficient, and scalable infrastructure that can meet the diverse needs of modern IoT applications.

2.(a) What is scalability in Cloud Computing? 10
Explain the following strategies of scaling:
(i) Proactive Scaling
(ii) Reactive Scaling
Ans: Scalability in cloud computing refers to the ability of a cloud infrastructure to handle an increasing or decreasing workload by dynamically adjusting its resources. Scalability ensures that a cloud-based system can grow to accommodate the increasing demands of users or applications, or shrink when demand decreases, without compromising performance, efficiency, or cost-effectiveness.

In the context of cloud computing, scalability is a key characteristic that allows organizations to efficiently manage resources and optimize costs while maintaining service availability and performance. There are two main types of scalabilities:

Vertical Scaling (Scaling Up): Adding more power to an existing server, such as increasing CPU, memory, or storage.

Horizontal Scaling (Scaling Out): Adding more instances of a server or resources, allowing for the distribution of the workload across multiple servers.

Strategies of Scaling

(i) Proactive Scaling

Proactive scaling involves anticipating changes in workload and scaling resources ahead of time to meet expected demand. This strategy is based on predictive analysis, historical data, and scheduled events. The goal is to ensure that resources are available when needed, without the delays that might occur with reactive scaling.

Key Features:

- **Predictive Analysis:** Using historical data and trends to predict future resource demands. For example, an e-commerce platform might increase resources before a scheduled sale or during holiday seasons when traffic spikes are expected.
- **Scheduled Scaling:** Resources are scaled based on predefined schedules, such as increasing resources every Monday morning when weekly traffic is typically higher.
- **Automation:** Proactive scaling often involves automation tools that adjust resources according to predictions or schedules without manual intervention.

Advantages:

- **Improved Performance:** By scaling resources in advance, proactive scaling can prevent performance degradation and ensure a smooth user experience during peak times.
- **Reduced Latency:** Resources are already in place when demand increases, minimizing response time and avoiding delays associated with scaling up.
- **Cost Management:** While proactive scaling can lead to increased resource usage, it can also prevent the costs associated with unexpected demand spikes and overloading.

Disadvantages:

Over-Provisioning: There is a risk of over-provisioning resources if the demand is overestimated, leading to unnecessary costs.

Complexity: Predicting demand accurately can be challenging, requiring sophisticated analytics and monitoring tools.

(ii) Reactive Scaling

Reactive scaling involves adjusting resources in response to actual changes in workload or demand. Unlike proactive scaling, which anticipates changes, reactive scaling monitors the system in real-time and scales resources up or down as needed, based on predefined rules or thresholds.

Key Features:

- **Real-Time Monitoring:** Reactive scaling relies on continuous monitoring of system metrics such as CPU usage, memory utilization, and network traffic.
- **Threshold-Based Scaling:** Resources are scaled based on specific triggers or thresholds. For example, if CPU usage exceeds 80%, additional instances are automatically added to handle the increased load.
- **Event-Driven:** Scaling actions are taken in response to specific events or conditions, such as a sudden spike in user traffic or an unexpected drop in performance.

Advantages:

- **Resource Efficiency:** Resources are only scaled when needed, reducing the risk of over-provisioning and minimizing costs.
- **Flexibility:** Reactive scaling can quickly adapt to unexpected changes in demand, ensuring that resources match the current workload.
- **Cost-Effectiveness:** By scaling resources only when necessary, reactive scaling can optimize costs by preventing unnecessary resource usage.

Disadvantages:
- **Latency:** There may be a delay in scaling up resources, especially if the demand spike is sudden, potentially leading to temporary performance degradation.
- **Unpredictability:** Reactive scaling depends on real-time events, which can make resource management less predictable compared to proactive scaling.

Both strategies have their advantages and disadvantages, and often, a combination of both (known as hybrid scaling) is used to balance performance, cost, and resource utilization effectively in cloud environments

(b) Define VM (Virtual Machine) sizing. Discuss the two ways to do VM sizing. 5

Ans: VM Sizing refers to the process of determining the appropriate amount of resources (such as CPU, memory, storage, and network bandwidth) to allocate to a virtual machine (VM) based on the specific needs of the applications or workloads that will run on it. Proper VM sizing is crucial for optimizing performance, ensuring efficient use of resources, and managing costs in a cloud or virtualized environment.

Two Ways to Do VM Sizing

1. Sizing Based on Application Requirements

This approach involves determining the VM size based on the specific resource requirements of the applications or workloads that will be running on the virtual machine. The goal is to allocate just enough resources to meet the application's needs without over-provisioning, which can lead to unnecessary costs.

Steps Involved:
- **Assess Application Needs:** Analyse the application's resource requirements, including CPU usage, memory consumption, storage needs, and network bandwidth. This can be done through profiling or by reviewing historical performance data.
- **Match with VM Templates:** Cloud providers and virtualization platforms typically offer predefined VM sizes (e.g., small, medium, large) with specific resource allocations. The application's requirements are matched to one of these predefined VM sizes.
- **Testing and Validation:** After selecting an initial VM size, the application should be tested to ensure it performs well under expected workloads. If necessary, adjustments can be made to the VM size.

Advantages:
- **Optimized Performance:** Ensures that the VM has sufficient resources to meet the application's needs, leading to optimal performance.
- **Cost-Efficiency:** By avoiding over-provisioning, this approach helps control costs, as only the necessary resources are allocated.

Disadvantages:
- **Complexity:** Requires detailed knowledge of the application's resource requirements, which can be time-consuming to gather and analyse.
- **Potential for Under-Sizing:** If the resource requirements are underestimated, the VM may be under-sized, leading to performance issues.

2. Sizing Based on Workload Analysis and Benchmarking

This approach involves analysing the workload that will run on the VM and using benchmarking tools to simulate the workload's behavior under different resource allocations. The objective is to empirically determine the optimal VM size by observing how the workload performs under various conditions.

Steps Involved:
- **Workload Characterization:** Understand the nature of the workload, including peak usage times, average resource consumption, and variability in demand. This can be done using monitoring tools and historical data analysis.
- **Benchmarking:** Use benchmarking tools to simulate the workload on VMs of different sizes. Measure performance metrics such as response time, throughput, CPU utilization, and memory usage.
- **Resource Allocation:** Based on the benchmarking results, select the VM size that provides the best balance between performance and cost. The VM size should handle the workload efficiently without over-allocating resources.

Advantages:
- **Data-Driven Decisions:** This approach uses empirical data to guide VM sizing decisions, reducing the risk of under- or over-sizing.
- **Scalability:** Workload analysis allows for more accurate forecasting of future resource needs, making it easier to scale VMs as the workload grows or changes.

Disadvantages:
- **Resource Intensive:** Benchmarking can be resource-intensive and time-consuming, especially for complex or variable workloads.
- **Initial Costs:** The process of running benchmarks and analysing workloads may involve upfront costs and time investment.

Both methods aim to achieve a balance between performance, resource utilization, and cost, depending on the specific use case and the nature of the workloads or applications.

(c) Mention any five applications of Cloud Computing. 5
Ans: Here are five key applications of cloud computing:

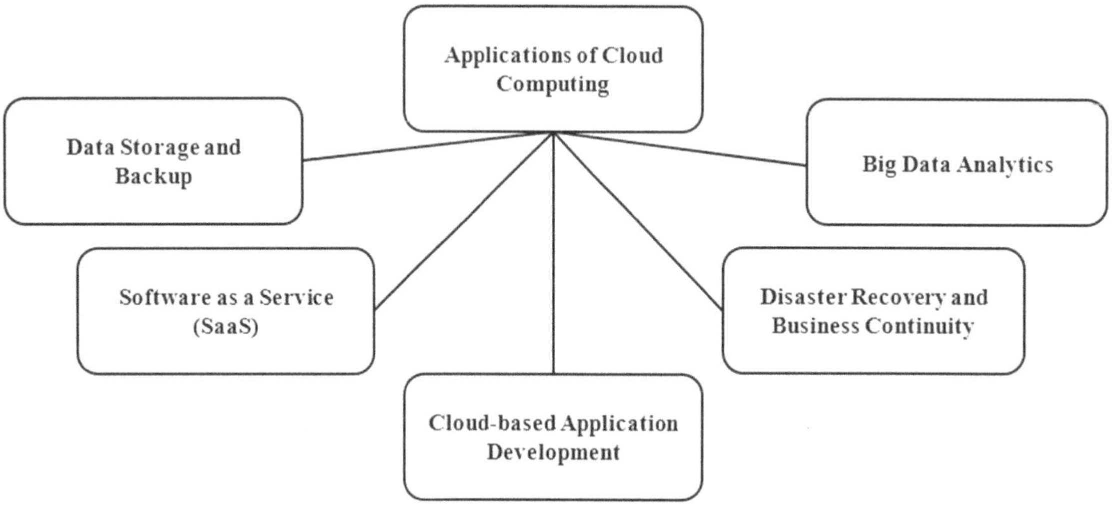

1. Data Storage and Backup
Cloud computing provides scalable and secure storage solutions where individuals and organizations can store large amounts of data. Popular services like Google Drive, Dropbox, and Amazon S3 offer cloud storage that allows users to access their data from any device with an internet connection. Additionally, cloud-based backup solutions help protect data by ensuring that it is automatically backed up and easily recoverable in the event of data loss.
2. Software as a Service (SaaS)
SaaS is one of the most common applications of cloud computing, where software applications are hosted on the cloud and made available to users over the internet. Examples include Microsoft Office 365, Salesforce, and Adobe Creative Cloud. Users can access these applications from any location without needing to install or maintain the software on their local devices.
3. Cloud-based Application Development
Developers use cloud computing to build, test, and deploy applications more efficiently. Platforms like AWS (Amazon Web Services), Microsoft Azure, and Google Cloud provide Infrastructure as a Service (IaaS) and Platform as a Service (PaaS) that offer a wide range of tools, frameworks, and services for developing scalable and robust applications without worrying about the underlying infrastructure.
4. Disaster Recovery and Business Continuity
Cloud computing enables organizations to implement effective disaster recovery solutions without the high cost associated with traditional on-premise solutions. Cloud-based disaster recovery services allow businesses to replicate

their data and IT systems in the cloud, ensuring quick recovery in case of hardware failures, natural disasters, or cyberattacks, thus maintaining business continuity.

5. Big Data Analytics

Cloud computing provides the processing power and storage necessary to handle big data analytics. Services like Amazon EMR, Google BigQuery, and Microsoft Azure HDInsight allow organizations to analyse vast amounts of data to gain insights and make data-driven decisions. This is particularly useful in industries such as finance, healthcare, and retail, where analysing large datasets can lead to improved customer experiences, operational efficiency, and competitive advantages.

These applications demonstrate the versatility and importance of cloud computing across various sectors, offering solutions that enhance efficiency, scalability, and accessibility.

3. (a) Define a sensor with reference to an IoT device. Explain various characteristics of sensors. Also, mention and explain any four classifications of sensors. 10

Ans: Define a Sensor with Reference to an IoT Device

Sensor Definition: In the context of an Internet of Things (IoT) device, a **sensor** is a hardware component that detects and measures physical properties or environmental conditions and converts these measurements into signals that can be interpreted by the IoT device or transmitted to other systems for processing and analysis. Sensors are crucial in IoT as they provide the data needed for devices to interact with their environment, make decisions, and trigger actions.

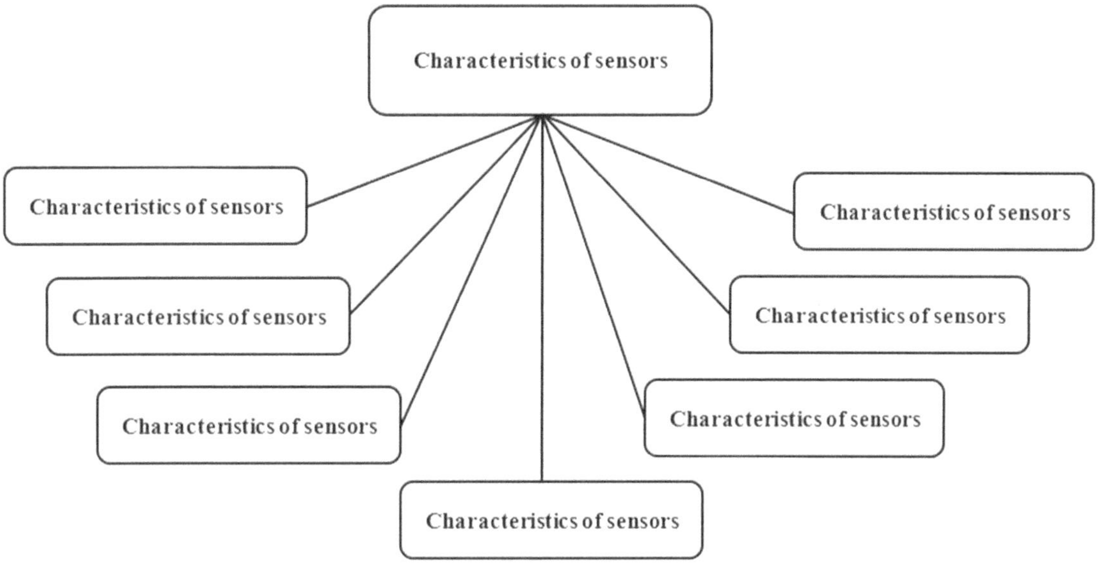

Characteristics of Sensors

1. Sensitivity:

Sensitivity refers to the sensor's ability to detect small changes in the physical property it is measuring. A highly sensitive sensor can detect even minimal variations in the environment, making it suitable for applications requiring precise measurements.

2. Accuracy:

Accuracy is the degree to which the sensor's measurements match the true value of the measured property. High accuracy is essential for applications where precise data is critical, such as in medical or industrial environments.

3. Range:

The range of a sensor is the span of values over which it can measure the physical property. For example, a temperature sensor might have a range of -50°C to 150°C. The range must be suitable for the application to ensure the sensor can effectively monitor the expected conditions.

4. Response Time:

Response time is the speed at which a sensor can detect a change in the measured property and provide an output. Fast response times are essential in applications where real-time data is crucial, such as in automotive safety systems.

5. Reliability:

Reliability refers to the sensor's ability to consistently perform its intended function over time without failure. Reliable sensors are essential in critical applications where consistent performance is required, such as in healthcare devices.

6. Durability:

Durability is the sensor's ability to withstand harsh environmental conditions, such as extreme temperatures, humidity, or mechanical stress. Sensors used in industrial or outdoor environments need to be durable to ensure long-term functionality.

7. Power Consumption:

Power consumption is an important characteristic, especially for battery-powered IoT devices. Sensors with low power consumption help extend the battery life of the device, making them ideal for remote or portable applications.

Classifications of Sensors

1. Based on the Type of Measured Property:

Temperature Sensors:

These sensors measure temperature or heat energy. Common examples include thermocouples, thermistors, and infrared temperature sensors. They are widely used in HVAC systems, industrial processes, and weather monitoring.

Pressure Sensors:

Pressure sensors measure the force exerted by a fluid (liquid or gas) on a surface. They are used in applications such as automotive, aerospace, and medical devices to monitor and control pressure levels.

2. Based on the Type of Output Signal:

Analog Sensors:

Analog sensors provide continuous signals that vary proportionally with the measured property. The output is typically a voltage or current that corresponds to the magnitude of the sensed variable. Examples include analog temperature sensors and light-dependent resistors (LDRs).

Digital Sensors:

Digital sensors provide discrete, digital output signals, usually in binary form (0 or 1), indicating the presence or absence of the measured property. These sensors are often used in applications requiring clear, binary decisions, such as motion detectors and digital thermometers.

3. Based on the Sensing Method:

Active Sensors:

Active sensors require an external power source to operate and typically generate an output signal in response to the measured property. Examples include LIDAR (Light Detection and Ranging) sensors, which emit light and measure the reflection to determine distances.

Passive Sensors:

Passive sensors do not require external power to operate; they detect and measure energy emitted by the environment or an object. Examples include thermocouples (which generate voltage based on temperature differences) and photodiodes (which generate current when exposed to light).

4. Based on the Physical Form:

Contact Sensors:

Contact sensors require direct physical contact with the measured property or object to detect changes. Examples include pressure sensors, strain gauges, and touch sensors. These are often used in applications like tactile sensing in robotics.

Non-Contact Sensors:

Non-contact sensors detect and measure properties without physical contact, often using electromagnetic fields, sound waves, or light. Examples include ultrasonic sensors, infrared sensors, and proximity sensors. These are widely used in automation, object detection, and security systems.

(b) Explain the following computing components used in laboratories of IoT/Cloud: 10

(i) Arduino

(ii) Raspberry Pi

Ans:

(i) Arduino

Arduino is an open-source electronics platform based on easy-to-use hardware and software. It consists of a microcontroller, which is a simple computer on a single integrated circuit that can be programmed to control various electronic components and devices. Arduino boards are widely used in IoT projects, educational settings, and hobbyist electronics because they are affordable, versatile, and easy to use.

Key Features:
- **Microcontroller-Based:** Arduino boards are equipped with microcontrollers (such as the ATmega328 on the Arduino Uno), which can be programmed to read inputs (such as sensors) and control outputs (such as motors or LEDs).
- **Open-Source Hardware and Software:** The Arduino platform includes both the physical hardware (the Arduino boards) and the Arduino Integrated Development Environment (IDE), which is used to write and upload code to the board. The open-source nature of Arduino has led to a large community of developers and extensive libraries for various applications.
- **Analog and Digital I/O:** Arduino boards typically have a combination of analog and digital input/output pins that can be used to connect a wide range of sensors, actuators, and other devices.
- **Connectivity Options:** Some Arduino models come with built-in connectivity options like Wi-Fi, Bluetooth, or Ethernet, making them suitable for IoT applications where devices need to communicate over a network.
- **Expandable:** Arduino boards can be expanded with additional modules or "shields" that add functionality, such as motor control, wireless communication, or additional I/O ports.

Applications in IoT:
- **Prototyping:** Arduino is widely used in prototyping IoT devices due to its simplicity and ease of use.
- **Sensor Data Collection:** Arduino can interface with various sensors to collect environmental data (e.g., temperature, humidity) and send it to cloud platforms for analysis.
- **Automation:** Arduino is often used in home automation projects, such as controlling lights, appliances, or security systems.

(ii) Raspberry Pi
Raspberry Pi is a low-cost, credit-card-sized single-board computer that can run a full-fledged operating system, such as Linux. It is designed to be an affordable and accessible platform for learning programming, electronics, and computer science. Due to its versatility and power, Raspberry Pi is commonly used in IoT and cloud-based projects, as well as in educational and industrial applications.

Key Features:
- **Full-Fledged Computer:** Unlike Arduino, which is a microcontroller, Raspberry Pi is a complete computer capable of running a full operating system, such as Raspberry Pi OS (based on Debian Linux), making it suitable for more complex tasks and applications.
- **Multiple I/O Ports:** Raspberry Pi has a variety of input/output ports, including USB ports, HDMI for video output, Ethernet for network connectivity, and GPIO (General Purpose Input/Output) pins for interfacing with sensors, actuators, and other hardware components.
- **Processing Power:** Raspberry Pi boards come with powerful processors (e.g., ARM-based CPUs) and sufficient memory to handle tasks like multimedia processing, web server hosting, and more. Some models also include Wi-Fi and Bluetooth connectivity.
- **Storage:** Raspberry Pi uses a microSD card for storage, where the operating system and data are stored. This makes it easy to upgrade or change the operating system as needed.
- **Community and Support:** Raspberry Pi has a large and active community that contributes to a wide range of projects, tutorials, and software, making it a popular choice for both beginners and advanced users.

Applications in IoT/Cloud:
- **Edge Computing:** Raspberry Pi can be used as an edge device in IoT applications, where it processes data locally before sending it to the cloud, reducing latency and bandwidth usage.
- **Home Automation:** Raspberry Pi is widely used in DIY home automation projects, controlling devices like lights, thermostats, and security cameras, often integrated with cloud services for remote management.
- **Media Center:** Raspberry Pi can be configured as a media center, streaming content from the cloud or local storage to various devices.
- **Educational Tool:** Raspberry Pi is extensively used in educational settings to teach programming, electronics, and computer science, often in the context of IoT projects.

Both platforms are essential tools in the development and experimentation of IoT and cloud technologies, each offering unique strengths that cater to different aspects of these fields.

4. (a) Discuss the following Service Delivery Models of Cloud, with an example for each: 10
(i) Platform as a Service (PaaS)
(ii) Infrastructure as a Service (IaaS)

Ans: Cloud computing offers various service delivery models that cater to different needs of users, ranging from software applications to infrastructure services. The two primary models are Platform as a Service (PaaS) and Infrastructure as a Service (IaaS).

(i) Platform as a Service (PaaS)

Platform as a Service (PaaS) is a cloud computing service model that provides a platform allowing customers to develop, run, and manage applications without dealing with the underlying infrastructure. PaaS supplies the necessary hardware, operating systems, and development tools in a pre-configured environment, enabling developers to focus on writing and deploying code rather than managing servers, storage, and networking.

Key Features:
- **Development Tools:** PaaS offers a set of tools and services for application development, including integrated development environments (IDEs), version control, testing tools, and deployment capabilities.
- **Scalability:** PaaS platforms automatically scale resources based on application demand, handling infrastructure scaling without developer intervention.
- **Middleware:** It often includes middleware that supports application services such as databases, messaging, and authentication.
- **Database Management:** PaaS providers typically offer managed database services, allowing developers to focus on the application logic rather than database maintenance.

Example:
- **Google App Engine:** Google App Engine is a PaaS offering that allows developers to build and deploy applications using a variety of programming languages (e.g., Python, Java, Node.js). It handles infrastructure concerns like load balancing, scaling, and monitoring, enabling developers to focus on writing code. App Engine automatically scales applications in response to traffic, ensuring high availability and performance.

(ii) Infrastructure as a Service (IaaS)

Infrastructure as a Service (IaaS) is a cloud computing service model that provides virtualized computing resources over the internet. It offers fundamental computing resources such as virtual machines (VMs), storage, networks, and load balancers. IaaS allows businesses to rent infrastructure on an as-needed basis, providing flexibility and scalability without the need to invest in physical hardware.

Key Features:
- **Virtualization:** IaaS uses virtualization technology to create and manage virtual machines, storage, and network resources that users can configure and manage according to their needs.
- **Scalability and Flexibility:** IaaS offers scalable resources that can be adjusted based on demand, enabling businesses to expand or contract their infrastructure as needed.
- **On-Demand Resources:** Users can provision and deprovision resources as needed, paying only for what they use, which provides cost efficiency.
- **Customizability:** IaaS allows users to configure and control the operating systems, storage, and applications running on their virtual infrastructure, offering a high degree of flexibility.

Example:
- **Amazon Web Services (AWS) EC2:** AWS Elastic Compute Cloud (EC2) is an IaaS offering that provides resizable compute capacity in the cloud. Users can launch virtual servers (instances) with various configurations of CPU, memory, and storage, and they can scale these instances up or down depending on their workload. EC2 allows users to choose their operating systems, install custom software, and control the entire environment, making it a highly flexible option for infrastructure needs.

These service delivery models enable organizations to leverage cloud computing according to their specific needs, whether they require a full development platform (PaaS) or raw computing infrastructure (IaaS).

(b) "Cloud Computing offers a variety of deployment models, a network connection viewpoint will be used to examine Cloud deployment models and their accessible components." With reference to this statement, discuss the following types of networks connectivities: 10

(i) Public Inter Cloud Networking

(ii) Private Intra Cloud Networking

Ans: Cloud computing offers various deployment models that define how cloud resources are managed, accessed, and used across different networks. The network connection viewpoint is crucial for understanding how cloud resources are interconnected, managed, and secured within these deployment models. The two types of network connectivity discussed here are Public Inter Cloud Networking and Private Intra Cloud Networking.

(i) Public Inter Cloud Networking

Public Inter Cloud Networking refers to the interconnection of multiple public cloud environments or the integration of public cloud resources with other cloud platforms or on-premises data centers. This type of connectivity enables data and services to be shared across different cloud providers or between a public cloud and other infrastructures.

Key Features:

- **Interoperability:** Public Inter Cloud Networking focuses on the seamless integration and interoperability between different public cloud services or providers, allowing organizations to leverage the strengths of multiple cloud platforms.
- **Data Transfer Across Clouds:** It enables the transfer of data and applications across various public cloud environments, supporting hybrid cloud strategies where workloads are distributed across multiple clouds.
- **Scalability and Flexibility:** Organizations can scale their infrastructure across multiple cloud providers, optimizing performance and cost by selecting the best cloud services for specific tasks.
- **Security Considerations:** Security in Public Inter Cloud Networking involves ensuring data protection during transit across different cloud environments and maintaining consistent security policies across all interconnected clouds.

Example:

- **Multi-Cloud Strategy:** An organization might use AWS for compute resources, Google Cloud for machine learning capabilities, and Azure for enterprise services. Public Inter Cloud Networking enables these clouds to communicate and share data securely, creating a cohesive and integrated cloud environment. For example, using AWS Direct Connect and Azure ExpressRoute, an organization can create private, high-bandwidth connections between AWS and Azure, enabling secure and efficient data transfer.

(ii) Private Intra Cloud Networking

Private Intra Cloud Networking refers to the internal networking within a single private cloud environment. This type of connectivity is designed for organizations that require dedicated, secure, and isolated cloud resources managed either on-premises or by a third-party provider. The focus is on the internal communication between virtual machines, storage, and other resources within the private cloud.

Key Features:

- **Isolation and Security:** Private Intra Cloud Networking provides a highly secure and isolated environment where all network traffic remains within the private cloud infrastructure. This is ideal for organizations with strict security, compliance, and data privacy requirements.
- **Custom Network Topologies:** Organizations can create customized network topologies tailored to their specific needs, such as segmented networks, VLANs (Virtual Local Area Networks), and VPNs (Virtual Private Networks), to control traffic flow and enhance security.
- **Control and Management:** Private Intra Cloud Networking allows organizations full control over their network configurations, including IP addressing, routing, firewalls, and access controls. This level of control is essential for maintaining compliance and optimizing performance.
- **Performance Optimization:** By keeping all network traffic within the private cloud, organizations can optimize performance, reduce latency, and improve reliability, especially for applications with high data throughput or low latency requirements.

Example:

- **On-Premises Private Cloud:** An organization might use a private cloud setup like VMware vSphere or OpenStack to manage its own data center resources. Private Intra Cloud Networking enables the organization to design its internal network, including secure communication between virtual machines, storage systems, and internal applications. For instance, the organization can create isolated network segments for different departments (e.g., HR, Finance, R&D) within the private cloud, ensuring that sensitive data is protected and that network traffic is efficiently managed.

These network connectivity models play a crucial role in determining how cloud resources are accessed, managed, and secured, depending on the specific needs and deployment strategies of the organization.

5. Write short notes on the following: 4*5=20
(a) Applications of Fog Computing
(b) Desktop Level Virtualization
(c) Actuator and it's any three types
(d) Zigbee, NFC and RFID connectivity technologies used in IoT applications.
Ans:

(a) Applications of Fog Computing
Fog Computing, also known as Edge Computing, is a decentralized computing infrastructure that extends cloud computing to the edge of the network, bringing data processing closer to the source of data generation. This approach reduces latency, conserves bandwidth, and enhances real-time data processing capabilities.

Applications:
1. Smart Cities:
Fog computing is used in smart cities to manage and analyze data from sensors deployed in infrastructure such as traffic lights, streetlights, and surveillance cameras. This enables real-time traffic management, efficient energy use, and improved public safety.
2. Industrial IoT (IIoT):
In industrial settings, fog computing processes data from machines and sensors on the factory floor in real-time, enabling predictive maintenance, quality control, and process optimization. It reduces the need to send all data to the cloud, minimizing latency and improving operational efficiency.
3. Autonomous Vehicles:
Fog computing allows autonomous vehicles to process sensor data locally, enabling quick decision-making for navigation, obstacle detection, and vehicle-to-vehicle communication. This is critical for ensuring the safety and reliability of autonomous systems.
4. Healthcare:
In healthcare, fog computing supports real-time monitoring and analysis of patient data from wearable devices, ensuring timely interventions in case of medical emergencies. It also supports telemedicine by enabling local processing of patient data, reducing latency in critical healthcare applications.
(b) Desktop Level Virtualization
Desktop Level Virtualization refers to the process of running a desktop operating system on a virtual machine (VM) that is hosted on a centralized server or cloud infrastructure. Users can access their virtual desktops remotely from any device, providing flexibility, security, and ease of management.

Key Aspects:
1. Virtual Desktop Infrastructure (VDI):
VDI is a desktop virtualization technology where desktop environments are hosted on virtual machines in a centralized data center. Users can access their desktops from any device with internet connectivity, allowing for flexible work environments and remote access.
2. Security and Management:
Desktop virtualization enhances security by centralizing desktop management and data storage. IT administrators can manage security policies, software updates, and backups from a central location, reducing the risk of data breaches and ensuring compliance with organizational policies.
3. Cost Efficiency:
By virtualizing desktops, organizations can reduce hardware costs, as users can access their virtual desktops using thin clients or lower-cost devices. It also reduces the need for hardware upgrades and maintenance.
4. Scalability:

Desktop virtualization allows organizations to scale their desktop environments quickly to meet changing demands. New virtual desktops can be provisioned and deployed rapidly, enabling faster onboarding of employees or support for temporary workloads.

(c) Actuator and Its Types

An actuator is a device that converts energy (usually electrical, hydraulic, or pneumatic) into mechanical motion to perform a physical action, such as moving, controlling, or adjusting a mechanism or system. Actuators are essential components in IoT devices, robotics, industrial automation, and various mechanical systems.

Types of Actuators:

1. Linear Actuators:

Linear actuators produce motion in a straight line and are commonly used in applications where linear movement is required. Examples include electric linear actuators used in adjustable beds, sliding doors, and robotics.

2. Rotary Actuators:

Rotary actuators produce rotational motion and are used in applications that require turning or spinning. Examples include electric motors, stepper motors, and servo motors used in robotics, conveyor belts, and industrial machinery.

3. Hydraulic Actuators:

Hydraulic actuators use fluid pressure to produce motion, typically providing powerful and precise control. They are commonly used in heavy machinery, such as construction equipment, aircraft control systems, and industrial presses.

4. Pneumatic Actuators:

Pneumatic actuators use compressed air to create motion and are often used in applications requiring quick, repetitive motion with lower force. Examples include pneumatic cylinders used in assembly lines, packaging machines, and automotive systems.

(d) Zigbee, NFC, and RFID Connectivity Technologies in IoT Applications

Zigbee:

Explanation: Zigbee is a low-power, low-data-rate wireless communication protocol designed for short-range communication. It is commonly used in IoT applications for home automation, smart lighting, and building control systems.

Applications: Zigbee is used in smart home devices like smart thermostats, lighting control systems, and security sensors. It supports mesh networking, allowing devices to communicate with each other and extend network coverage.

NFC (Near Field Communication):

Explanation: NFC is a short-range wireless communication technology that enables data exchange between devices within a few centimeters. It operates at a high frequency and is primarily used for secure, contactless transactions.

Applications: NFC is widely used in mobile payment systems (e.g., Apple Pay, Google Pay), access control (e.g., contactless entry systems), and data sharing between devices (e.g., pairing Bluetooth devices or sharing contact information).

RFID (Radio Frequency Identification):

Explanation: RFID is a wireless technology that uses electromagnetic fields to automatically identify and track tags attached to objects. RFID systems consist of a reader and tags, which can be passive or active.

Applications: RFID is used in inventory management, supply chain logistics, asset tracking, and access control systems. For example, RFID tags are attached to products in a warehouse, allowing for automated inventory tracking and management.

MCS – 227

Master Of Computer Applications (MCA)
Chapter 3: Term-End Examination, June, 2023
MCS-227: Cloud Computing and Iot

Time: 3 Hours
Maximum Marks: 100
Weightage: 70
Note: Question No. 1 is compulsory. Answer any three Questions from the rest.

1. (a) What is cloud computing service delivery models? List and explain any four service delivery models. 10
Ans: Cloud Computing Service Delivery Models refer to the different ways in which cloud services are provided to users. These models define the scope of services offered by the cloud provider, ranging from basic infrastructure to fully managed applications. The service delivery models help organizations select the level of control, flexibility, and management they require over their IT resources.

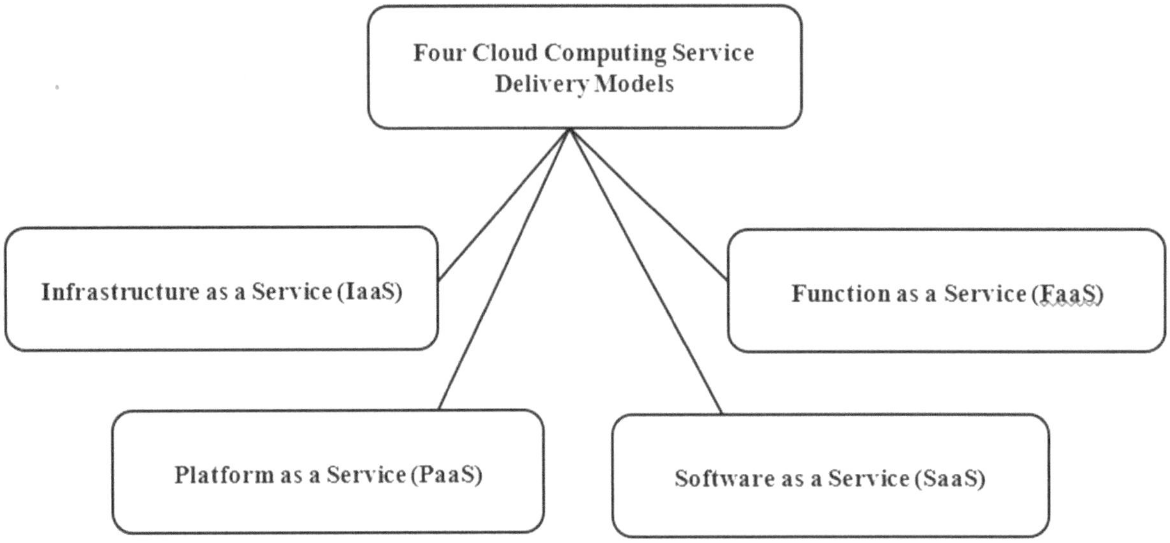

Four Cloud Computing Service Delivery Models
1. Infrastructure as a Service (IaaS)
Infrastructure as a Service (IaaS) is the most basic cloud service model. It provides virtualized computing resources over the internet, including servers, storage, and networking. Users can rent these resources on a pay-as-you-go basis, which allows them to scale infrastructure up or down according to their needs.

Key Features:
- **Virtual Machines:** Users can create and manage virtual servers with the operating systems and applications of their choice.
- **Scalability:** IaaS allows for dynamic scaling of resources, making it ideal for workloads that require flexibility.
- **Control:** Users have control over the operating system, storage, and installed applications, providing a high level of customization.

Example: Amazon Web Services (AWS) EC2, Microsoft Azure Virtual Machines, Google Compute Engine.

2. Platform as a Service (PaaS)

Platform as a Service (PaaS) provides a platform and environment for developers to build, test, and deploy applications without worrying about the underlying infrastructure. PaaS includes tools, libraries, and services that simplify the development process, allowing developers to focus on writing code.

Key Features:
- **Development Tools:** PaaS provides integrated development environments (IDEs), frameworks, and middleware to streamline application development.
- **Managed Infrastructure:** The cloud provider manages the underlying infrastructure, including servers, storage, and networking, as well as runtime environments.
- **Scalability:** PaaS platforms can automatically scale applications based on demand, ensuring high availability and performance.

Example: Google App Engine, Microsoft Azure App Services, Heroku.

3. Software as a Service (SaaS)
Software as a Service (SaaS) delivers fully functional applications over the internet. These applications are managed and maintained by the cloud provider, and users access them through a web browser or an application interface. SaaS is ideal for organizations that need ready-to-use software without the burden of installation, maintenance, or updates.

Key Features:
- **Accessibility:** SaaS applications can be accessed from any device with an internet connection, offering convenience and mobility.
- **Subscription-Based:** Users typically pay for SaaS applications on a subscription basis, which can be monthly or yearly, reducing upfront costs.
- **Automatic Updates:** The cloud provider handles all updates, security patches, and maintenance, ensuring that users always have access to the latest version of the software.

Example: Microsoft Office 365, Google Workspace (formerly G Suite), Salesforce.

4. Function as a Service (FaaS)
Function as a Service (FaaS) is a serverless computing model where developers can execute code in response to events without provisioning or managing servers. FaaS platforms automatically scale resources based on the demand for the function, and users are charged only for the actual execution time of their code.

Key Features:
- **Event-Driven Execution:** Functions are triggered by specific events, such as HTTP requests, database changes, or messages in a queue.
- **No Server Management:** The cloud provider manages all infrastructure, allowing developers to focus solely on writing code.
- **Cost-Efficiency:** Users only pay for the time their code is running, making FaaS a cost-effective solution for applications with unpredictable workloads.

Example: AWS Lambda, Google Cloud Functions, Microsoft Azure Functions.

These service delivery models cater to different needs and levels of control, allowing organizations to choose the model that best fits their specific requirements and operational goals.

(b) Explain the following scaling strategies: 10
(i) Proactive scaling
(ii) Reactive scaling
(iii) Combinational scaling
Also, compare proactive and reactive scaling with reference to the suitability, working, cost and implementation parameters.
Ans: Scaling strategies in cloud computing or data management are essential techniques that help systems adapt to varying workloads and demands. Here's an explanation of three key scaling strategies:

(i) Proactive Scaling

Proactive scaling is a strategy where scaling decisions are made in advance based on predicted workloads. It involves analysing historical data, forecasting future demand, and scheduling scaling actions accordingly. The main objective is to prevent performance issues before they occur by scaling resources up or down at predetermined times or in response to forecasted conditions.

Working:

Proactive scaling uses predictive analytics and machine learning models to forecast traffic or demand spikes. Based on these predictions, additional resources are provisioned in advance. For example, an e-commerce site might scale up its resources before a big sale event based on past trends.

Suitability:

This approach is particularly suitable for applications with predictable workloads or recurring patterns, such as seasonal business trends or regular traffic spikes.

Cost:

Proactive scaling can be cost-effective if predictions are accurate, as it avoids over-provisioning during low-demand periods and ensures sufficient resources during high-demand times. However, incorrect predictions can lead to unnecessary costs.

Implementation:

Implementing proactive scaling requires robust data analytics capabilities and the ability to integrate forecasting tools with the cloud management platform.

(ii) Reactive Scaling

Reactive scaling is a strategy where scaling actions are taken in response to real-time changes in demand. It involves monitoring system performance metrics (e.g., CPU usage, memory utilization) and triggering scaling actions when these metrics cross predefined thresholds.

Working:

Reactive scaling relies on real-time monitoring tools that continuously assess the system's current state. When the system experiences high load (e.g., CPU usage exceeds 80%), additional resources are automatically provisioned. Conversely, when the load decreases, excess resources are de-provisioned.

Suitability:

Reactive scaling is suitable for applications with unpredictable or fluctuating workloads, where it's challenging to forecast demand accurately. It's ideal for scenarios where immediate response to workload changes is necessary.

Cost:

Reactive scaling can be more expensive than proactive scaling because it involves dynamic scaling in response to unexpected demand surges, which might lead to temporary over-provisioning. However, it avoids the risks of under-provisioning.

Implementation:

This strategy is easier to implement than proactive scaling because it relies on straightforward metrics and triggers. However, it requires a robust monitoring and automation system to respond quickly to changes.

(iii) Combinational Scaling

Combinational scaling combines proactive and reactive scaling strategies to leverage the benefits of both approaches. It uses predictive analytics to schedule scaling actions while also responding to real-time demand changes.

Working:

In combinational scaling, a baseline of resources is allocated based on predictions (proactive). If real-time metrics indicate a significant deviation from the predicted load, reactive scaling triggers additional adjustments. This ensures that resources are always optimized, balancing performance and cost.

Suitability:
This strategy is suitable for applications with both predictable and unpredictable workloads. It provides a balanced approach that can handle various scenarios effectively.

Cost:
Combinational scaling aims to optimize costs by using predictions to avoid unnecessary scaling while still ensuring resources are available for sudden demand changes. However, it can be more complex and expensive to implement due to the need for both predictive analytics and real-time monitoring.

Implementation:
Implementing combinational scaling requires a sophisticated setup that integrates both proactive and reactive elements. It demands advanced analytics capabilities and responsive monitoring systems.

Comparison of Proactive and Reactive Scaling

Parameter	Proactive Scaling	Reactive Scaling
Suitability	Best for predictable workloads with clear demand patterns.	Ideal for unpredictable, fluctuating workloads.
Working	Uses forecasts to scale resources in advance.	Monitors real-time metrics to trigger scaling actions.
Cost	Can be cost-effective if predictions are accurate.	May incur higher costs due to dynamic scaling needs.
Implementation	Requires predictive analytics and integration with cloud.	Easier to implement; requires real-time monitoring and automation.

Proactive scaling is advantageous when demand patterns are predictable, offering potential cost savings with accurate forecasting. Reactive scaling, on the other hand, excels in handling unexpected demand fluctuations but may lead to higher costs due to its on-demand nature. Combinational scaling, while complex, provides a balanced approach to managing both predictable and unpredictable workloads.

(c) Explain all the four components, which support IoT system, with the help of a sample block diagram. 10
Ans: An Internet of Things (IoT) system comprises several key components that work together to collect, process, and analyse data, as well as to trigger actions. These components are essential for creating an interconnected environment where devices can communicate with each other and with centralized systems, providing valuable insights and automation.

Four Key Components of an IoT System
- **Sensors/Devices**
- **Connectivity**
- **Data Processing**
- **User Interface**

Let's discuss each component in detail, followed by a sample block diagram that illustrates how these components interact in an IoT system.

1. Sensors/Devices
Sensors or devices are the "things" in the Internet of Things. They are responsible for collecting data from the environment, such as temperature, humidity, motion, light, or pressure. In addition to sensors, devices can include actuators that perform actions based on received instructions, like turning on a light or opening a valve.

Function:
- **Data Collection:** Sensors gather real-time data from the environment, which can be sent to the system for further processing.
- **Interaction with the Environment:** Devices like actuators can respond to commands and interact with the physical world by performing specific actions.

Example:

- A temperature sensor that measures the temperature in a room.
- A smart thermostat that adjusts the heating or cooling system based on the sensor data.

2. Connectivity

Connectivity refers to the communication between sensors/devices and other components of the IoT system, such as data processing units or cloud servers. This communication can occur over various networks, such as Wi-Fi, Bluetooth, Zigbee, cellular networks, or Ethernet.

Function:

- **Data Transmission:** Connectivity ensures that the data collected by sensors is transmitted to the data processing unit or cloud platform for analysis.
- **Protocol Management:** Different communication protocols (e.g., MQTT, HTTP, CoAP) are used to ensure reliable and efficient data transmission between devices and the central system.

Example:

- A smart home system where sensors communicate with a central hub over Wi-Fi.
- A wearable fitness tracker that sends data to a mobile app via Bluetooth.

3. Data Processing

Data processing is the component where the collected data is analysed and processed to generate meaningful insights. This processing can happen locally (on edge devices), at an intermediate layer (fog computing), or in the cloud. The data processing component is responsible for filtering, aggregating, and analysing the data to enable decision-making.

Function:

- **Data Analysis:** The raw data collected by sensors is processed and analysed to identify patterns, trends, or anomalies.
- **Real-Time Decision Making:** In some cases, data processing needs to occur in real-time to trigger immediate actions, such as sending alerts or activating actuators.

Example:

- A cloud platform that analyses temperature data from multiple sensors to detect potential overheating in a factory.
- Edge computing where a local gateway processes sensor data to control a machine in real-time.

4. User Interface

The user interface (UI) is the component that allows users to interact with the IoT system. It could be a dashboard, mobile app, web application, or any other interface that provides users with insights, notifications, and control over the IoT system. The UI is critical for monitoring the system, configuring devices, and making informed decisions based on the data collected and processed.

Function:

- **Data Visualization:** The UI displays the processed data in a user-friendly format, such as graphs, charts, or alerts, enabling users to understand the system's status and trends.
- **System Control:** Users can control IoT devices, set thresholds, and configure the system via the UI, allowing for a more interactive and responsive experience.

Example:

- A mobile app that shows the current temperature in different rooms of a smart home and allows the user to adjust the thermostat settings.
- A web dashboard that visualizes energy consumption data for an industrial plant and enables remote control of equipment.

Sample Block Diagram of an IoT System

Below is a conceptual block diagram that illustrates the interaction between the four key components of an IoT system:

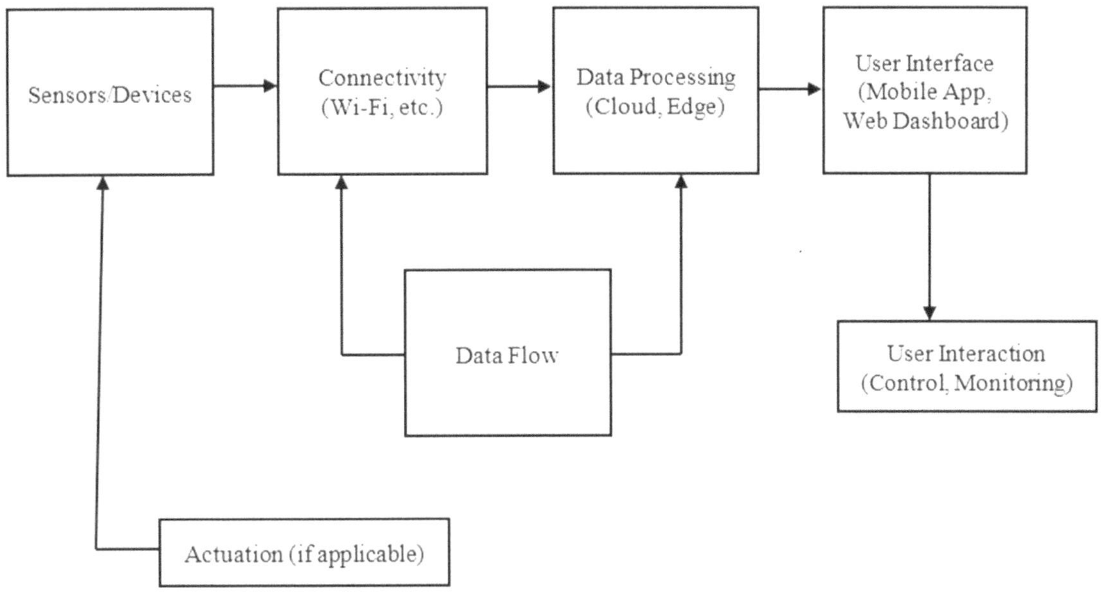

Explanation of the Diagram:
- **Sensors/Devices** collect data from the environment and send it to the **Connectivity** component.
- The **Connectivity** component transmits this data to the **Data Processing** unit, which can be located at the edge, in the fog layer, or in the cloud.
- The **Data Processing** unit analyses the data and generates actionable insights, which are then communicated to the **User Interface**.
- The **User Interface** allows users to visualize the data, monitor the system, and control devices as needed.

This interconnected system enables IoT solutions to operate efficiently, providing real-time monitoring, analysis, and control over a wide range of applications.

(d) What is fog computing? Explain the working of its along with any use case. Also, mention it advantages. 10

Ans: Fog Computing is a decentralized computing infrastructure that extends cloud computing to the edge of the network. It involves processing data closer to where it is generated, such as on local devices or edge servers, rather than sending it to a centralized cloud for processing. Fog computing aims to reduce latency, conserve bandwidth, and enhance real-time data processing capabilities, making it particularly suitable for applications that require immediate response times and low latency.

Working of Fog Computing
Fog computing operates by placing intermediary processing nodes, known as fog nodes, between IoT devices and the central cloud. These fog nodes can be located at the edge of the network, near the data source, and can process data locally or in conjunction with the cloud.

Steps in Fog Computing:
1. Data Generation:
IoT devices, such as sensors and actuators, generate vast amounts of data from their interactions with the environment. This data can include temperature readings, motion detection, video feeds, etc.
2. Data Transmission:
The generated data is transmitted to a nearby fog node, which could be a local server, router, gateway, or even an edge device with sufficient computing power.
3. Local Processing:

The fog node processes the data locally, performing tasks such as filtering, aggregation, analysis, and decision-making. This local processing reduces the amount of data that needs to be sent to the cloud, minimizing latency and bandwidth usage.

4. Action Execution:
Based on the processed data, the fog node can trigger immediate actions, such as activating an actuator, sending alerts, or adjusting device settings. If further processing is required, the fog node can forward the data to the cloud.

5. Cloud Interaction:
The fog node communicates with the cloud for more complex data processing, long-term storage, or analytics that cannot be handled locally. The cloud can also send instructions back to the fog node based on its analysis.

6. User Interaction:
Users can interact with the system through a user interface, such as a mobile app or web dashboard, which provides insights and control over the devices and data.

Use Case of Fog Computing:
Smart Traffic Management: In a smart city, traffic management systems need to monitor and control traffic flow in real-time to reduce congestion, manage traffic signals, and ensure road safety. Sensors installed at intersections and along roads collect data on vehicle speed, traffic density, and pedestrian movement.

Working:
- **Data Collection:** Sensors and cameras collect real-time data on traffic conditions, including the number of vehicles, their speeds, and the presence of pedestrians.
- **Local Processing (Fog Nodes):** Fog nodes, located at traffic intersections or within the city's network, process this data locally. They analyse traffic patterns, predict congestion, and adjust traffic signals dynamically to optimize flow.
- **Immediate Actions:** Based on the processed data, the fog nodes can adjust traffic lights in real-time, control pedestrian crossings, and send alerts to drivers about potential hazards or alternative routes.
- **Cloud Interaction:** Aggregated data from multiple fog nodes is sent to the cloud for long-term analysis, such as identifying patterns over time, planning infrastructure improvements, or optimizing traffic management strategies.
- **User Interaction:** City traffic managers and residents can access real-time traffic information through a mobile app, allowing them to make informed decisions about their travel routes.

Advantages of Fog Computing

1. Reduced Latency:
Fog computing processes data closer to the source, significantly reducing the time it takes to make decisions. This is crucial for applications that require real-time responses, such as autonomous vehicles, industrial automation, or smart traffic management.

2. Bandwidth Efficiency:
By processing data locally and only sending relevant or aggregated data to the cloud, fog computing conserves bandwidth. This reduces the need for high-capacity data transmission and lowers costs associated with data transfer.

3. Enhanced Security and Privacy:
Fog computing allows for sensitive data to be processed and stored locally, reducing the need to transmit it over potentially insecure networks. This enhances data privacy and security, as local data processing can adhere to specific security protocols.

4. Scalability:
Fog computing enables scalable solutions by distributing processing tasks across multiple fog nodes. As demand grows, additional fog nodes can be added to handle increased workloads, allowing for flexible and scalable infrastructure.

5. Reliability and Resilience:
With fog computing, the system can continue to operate even if the connection to the central cloud is lost. Local processing ensures that critical tasks can be performed without relying on constant cloud connectivity, enhancing the overall resilience of the system.

6. Improved Decision-Making:
The ability to process data in real-time at the edge allows for more immediate and accurate decision-making, which is essential in time-sensitive applications like healthcare monitoring or emergency response systems.

These benefits make fog computing an essential component in the architecture of modern IoT systems, particularly in applications requiring low latency and high responsiveness.

2. (a) Define edge computing. Also, briefly explain the working of edge computing. **10**

Ans: Edge Computing is a distributed computing paradigm that brings computation and data storage closer to the location where it is needed, typically at or near the source of data generation, such as IoT devices, sensors, or local servers. Instead of relying solely on centralized cloud data centers, edge computing processes data locally, reducing the need to transmit large volumes of data to the cloud. This approach helps to minimize latency, conserve bandwidth, and enable real-time processing and decision-making.

Working of Edge Computing

Edge computing operates by deploying computing resources, such as servers, gateways, or embedded systems, at the edge of the network,near the data source. The primary goal is to process data locally to avoid the delays and bandwidth usage associated with sending data to centralized cloud servers for processing. Here's how edge computing works:

1. Data Generation:

Data Sources: IoT devices, sensors, cameras, and other data-generating devices produce large amounts of data in real-time. For example, a security camera in a smart building continuously captures video footage, or a sensor in an industrial machine monitors temperature and vibration.

2. Data Transmission:

Local Transmission: The data generated by these devices is transmitted to nearby edge devices, such as edge servers, gateways, or embedded systems, rather than being sent directly to a central cloud data center. This proximity enables faster data transmission with lower latency.

3. Local Processing:

Computation at the Edge: The edge devices process the incoming data locally. This processing can include tasks such as filtering, aggregating, analysing, or applying machine learning algorithms to the data. For example, an edge server might analyse video footage from a security camera to detect suspicious activities in real-time.

4. Immediate Actions:

Real-Time Decision-Making: Based on the processed data, the edge devices can take immediate actions or trigger responses. For instance, if the edge device detects an anomaly in an industrial machine, it can immediately shut down the machine to prevent damage.

5. Data Forwarding (Optional):

Sending Data to the Cloud: After processing data locally, edge devices can selectively forward relevant data to the cloud for further analysis, storage, or long-term decision-making. This reduces the amount of data sent to the cloud, conserving bandwidth and lowering costs.

6. User Interaction:

Monitoring and Control: Users can interact with the system through user interfaces such as mobile apps, dashboards, or web portals. They can monitor the status of the devices, receive alerts, and make adjustments as needed.

Edge computing is essential for applications that require real-time responses, such as autonomous vehicles, industrial automation, smart cities, and healthcare monitoring systems. By processing data at the edge, these applications can operate more efficiently and effectively, even in environments where cloud connectivity is limited or unreliable.

(b) What is Virtualization? Explain its underlying abstraction. Also, mention important characteristics. 10

Ans: Virtualization is a technology that allows for the creation of a virtual version of something, such as hardware, storage, networks, or even entire computing environments, using specialized software. In essence, virtualization enables multiple virtual instances of resources or environments to run on a single physical system. This process abstracts the physical hardware, allowing multiple operating systems and applications to run concurrently on the same machine, each within its isolated environment.

Underlying Abstraction of Virtualization

The underlying abstraction in virtualization involves separating the physical hardware from the operating system and applications. This is achieved using a layer of software called a **hypervisor** (also known as a virtual machine monitor, or VMM). The hypervisor sits between the physical hardware and the virtual machines (VMs), managing the distribution of physical resources (such as CPU, memory, and storage) among the VMs.

How It Works:
- **Physical Layer:** The physical hardware includes the server, storage devices, network interfaces, and other computing resources.
- **Hypervisor Layer:** The hypervisor is the software layer that abstracts the physical hardware. It creates and manages multiple virtual machines on the host system. Each virtual machine acts as an independent system, with its operating system and applications.
- **Virtual Machines (VMs):** Each VM operates independently and is isolated from other VMs, even though they share the same physical hardware. The hypervisor allocates resources to each VM as needed, balancing workloads and optimizing resource use.

This abstraction allows for greater flexibility, resource efficiency, and scalability. It also enables features like live migration (moving VMs between hosts without downtime), snapshots (capturing the state of a VM at a specific point in time), and fault tolerance.

Important Characteristics of Virtualization
1. Isolation:
Each virtual machine operates in a completely isolated environment, meaning that the activities within one VM do not affect other VMs on the same physical host. This isolation is crucial for security, stability, and reliability, as it prevents one VM's issues from impacting others.
2. Resource Efficiency:
Virtualization allows for better utilization of physical resources by enabling multiple virtual machines to share the same hardware. This reduces the need for physical servers, leading to cost savings on hardware, power, cooling, and space.
3. Scalability:
Virtualization provides the ability to easily scale up or down by creating new virtual machines or adjusting the resources allocated to existing ones. This scalability is crucial in dynamic environments where workloads can vary significantly.
4. Flexibility:
Virtualization allows for the quick deployment of new environments and applications. VMs can be easily cloned, migrated, or adjusted without significant downtime or reconfiguration of physical hardware.
5. Portability:
Virtual machines can be moved between different physical hosts with minimal disruption. This portability allows for load balancing, disaster recovery, and ease of management across multiple data centers or cloud environments.
6. Improved Disaster Recovery:
Virtualization enables easier and more efficient backup and disaster recovery processes. Virtual machines can be backed up, replicated, and restored more quickly than physical servers, minimizing downtime in case of hardware failures.
7. Hardware Independence:
Virtualization decouples the operating system and applications from the underlying hardware, allowing VMs to be moved or copied to different physical machines without compatibility issues.
8. Dynamic Resource Allocation:
The hypervisor can dynamically allocate resources such as CPU, memory, and storage to VMs based on their needs. This dynamic allocation ensures that resources are used efficiently and that VMs can perform optimally.

These characteristics make virtualization a foundational technology for modern IT infrastructure, enabling cloud computing, efficient resource management, and improved system reliability.

3. (a) Compare and contrast cluster, grid and cloud computing with reference to physical characteristics, structure, hardware, resources, applications, networking and scalability parameters. 10
Ans: Cluster, grid, and cloud computing are three different paradigms used to solve computational problems and provide resources for various applications. Each of these paradigms has its own set of characteristics, structure, hardware requirements, resource management approaches, applications, networking, and scalability features. Below is a detailed comparison and contrast of these three computing models:

Parameter	Cluster Computing	Grid Computing	Cloud Computing
Physical Characteristics	- Typically located in a single location (data center) - Homogeneous hardware setup (similar processors, memory, etc.)	- Distributed across multiple locations - Heterogeneous hardware setup (different processors, storage, etc.)	- Highly distributed and can span across multiple data centers globally - Heterogeneous hardware setup
Structure	- Tightly coupled nodes in a single physical location - Nodes are connected via a high-speed local area network (LAN)	- Loosely coupled, geographically dispersed systems - Nodes are connected via a wide area network (WAN) or the internet	- Highly abstracted from physical hardware - Resources are provided as a service over the internet
Hardware	- Identical or similar hardware configurations - Typically uses specialized, high-performance hardware (e.g., supercomputers)	- Diverse and heterogeneous hardware configurations - Utilizes standard, commodity hardware	- Virtualized hardware - Flexible, scalable infrastructure with various types of virtual machines and storage options
Resources	- Shared resources (CPU, memory, storage) among nodes - Managed and coordinated by a central management system (e.g., cluster manager)	- Aggregated resources from multiple locations - Managed by a distributed resource management system (e.g., middleware)	- Virtualized resources abstracted from physical hardware - Managed by cloud service providers with dynamic allocation
Applications	- High-performance computing (HPC) applications - Scientific simulations, financial modeling, and research computations	- Large-scale computations requiring vast distributed resources - Scientific research, complex simulations, and collaborative projects	- Web applications, data analytics, machine learning, and general-purpose computing - Scalable enterprise applications, SaaS, PaaS, IaaS
Networking	- High-speed LAN (e.g., InfiniBand, Ethernet) for communication between nodes - Low-latency network with high bandwidth	- Internet or WAN for communication between geographically dispersed nodes - May experience higher latency compared to clusters	- Internet-based networking with varying latencies depending on the geographic location of data centers - Scalable network infrastructure with load balancing
Scalability	- Limited scalability, typically confined to the number of nodes in the cluster - Scaling requires adding more nodes to the cluster, often within the same data center	- High scalability across multiple locations - Can leverage vast numbers of nodes, but scalability may be limited by network bandwidth and coordination overhead	- Highly scalable with virtually unlimited resources - Can scale dynamically based on demand, with the ability to add or remove resources as needed (elastic scalability)

Key Comparisons:

1. Physical Characteristics:

Cluster Computing: Usually involves a group of similar or identical computers located in the same physical location, interconnected by a high-speed network.

Grid Computing: Consists of a network of distributed and often geographically separated computers that work together, which may have different hardware configurations.

Cloud Computing: Provides highly distributed, virtualized resources that can be accessed over the internet. The physical hardware is abstracted away from the user.

2. Structure:
Cluster Computing: Tightly coupled systems within a single data center, with a centralized management system.
Grid Computing: Loosely coupled systems spread across multiple locations, often connected through the internet or WAN.
Cloud Computing: Highly abstracted, offering resources as services over the internet, with a focus on scalability and flexibility.
3. Hardware:
Cluster Computing: Uses specialized and often identical hardware configurations optimized for high-performance computing.
Grid Computing: Involves diverse and heterogeneous hardware configurations, utilizing standard, often commodity, hardware across different locations.
Cloud Computing: Employs virtualized hardware, allowing for flexible resource allocation and usage based on demand.
4. Resources:
Cluster Computing: Resources such as CPU, memory, and storage are tightly managed and shared among the nodes in the cluster.
Grid Computing: Aggregates resources from multiple, geographically dispersed locations, coordinated by distributed middleware.
Cloud Computing: Provides virtualized resources abstracted from the physical hardware, managed dynamically by cloud service providers.
5. Applications:
Cluster Computing: Best suited for high-performance computing applications that require significant processing power, such as scientific simulations.
Grid Computing: Ideal for large-scale computations and projects that need to harness the collective power of distributed resources.
Cloud Computing: Supports a wide range of applications, from simple web services to complex machine learning models and enterprise solutions.
6. Networking:
Cluster Computing: Relies on a high-speed, low-latency LAN for communication between nodes.
Grid Computing: Uses the internet or WAN, which may have higher latency and lower bandwidth compared to cluster networking.
Cloud Computing: Operates over the internet, with scalable network infrastructure that can handle varying latencies and load.
7. Scalability:
Cluster Computing: Limited scalability, often constrained by the physical limits of the cluster's data center.
Grid Computing: Offers higher scalability by leveraging resources across multiple locations, though it may face challenges related to coordination and network performance.
Cloud Computing: Provides virtually unlimited scalability with the ability to dynamically scale resources up or down based on demand.

Each model has its specific use cases, strengths, and challenges, depending on the computational requirements and the nature of the tasks at hand.

(b) What is load balancing? What is its functionality? Explain the following load-balancers along with their features: 10

(i) Network load balancer
(ii) Application load balancer
Ans: Load Balancing is a process used in computing and networking to distribute incoming network traffic or workloads across multiple servers or resources to ensure no single server or resource is overwhelmed. The primary goal of load balancing is to optimize resource use, maximize throughput, minimize response time, and ensure reliability and availability of applications or services. By evenly distributing the load, load balancing prevents server overloads, reduces the chances of downtime, and enhances the overall performance of the system.

Functionality of Load Balancing
The key functionalities of load balancing include:

1. Traffic Distribution: Load balancers distribute incoming client requests or network traffic evenly across multiple servers, ensuring that no single server bears too much load.
2. Health Monitoring: Load balancers continuously monitor the health and availability of servers. If a server goes down or becomes unresponsive, the load balancer redirects traffic to the healthy servers, ensuring continuous service availability.
3. Fault Tolerance: By distributing traffic across multiple servers, load balancing adds redundancy to the system, ensuring that even if one server fails, others can take over the load, thus preventing service disruption.
4. Scalability: Load balancers allow systems to scale easily by adding or removing servers as demand changes. As traffic increases, more servers can be added to handle the additional load.
5. Session Persistence: Load balancers can manage sessions by ensuring that requests from the same client are directed to the same server, maintaining session continuity.
6. SSL Termination: Some load balancers handle SSL encryption and decryption, offloading this resource-intensive task from application servers, which improves performance.

Types of Load Balancers
(i) Network Load Balancer (NLB)
A Network Load Balancer operates at the Transport Layer (Layer 4) of the OSI model. It is designed to handle large volumes of traffic and distribute it based on network information such as IP address and TCP/UDP ports. NLBs are highly efficient for load balancing at the protocol level and are well-suited for high-performance, low-latency traffic management.

Features:
- **Protocol-Based Routing:** NLBs use protocol-level information (such as IP address and port numbers) to distribute traffic. They do not inspect the actual content of the traffic, making them faster and more efficient for handling high throughput.
- **High Throughput:** NLBs are optimized for handling large amounts of simultaneous requests and can scale to support millions of requests per second.
- **Low Latency:** Since NLBs operate at a lower network layer, they add minimal latency to the request processing, making them suitable for applications where speed is critical.
- **Connection Persistence:** NLBs can maintain session persistence (also known as "sticky sessions") by keeping track of client-server connections and ensuring that subsequent requests from the same client are sent to the same server.
- **Health Checks:** NLBs perform regular health checks on servers to ensure they are available and capable of handling requests. If a server fails, the NLB will route traffic to healthy servers.

Use Cases:
High-performance applications requiring low latency and high throughput, such as gaming servers, real-time financial applications, and large-scale web services.

(ii) Application Load Balancer (ALB)
An Application Load Balancer operates at the Application Layer (Layer 7) of the OSI model. ALBs are more sophisticated than NLBs because they can inspect the content of the incoming traffic, making decisions based on the HTTP headers, URL paths, or other request attributes. This makes ALBs ideal for managing web traffic and routing requests based on application-specific criteria.

Features:
- **Content-Based Routing:** ALBs can route traffic based on specific content within the HTTP request, such as the URL path, host headers, or cookies. This allows for more advanced traffic management, such as directing users to different servers based on the content they are requesting.
- **Advanced Load Balancing Algorithms:** ALBs support more complex algorithms like round-robin, least connections, and IP hash, which distribute traffic based on various factors, such as server load or client IP address.
- **SSL Termination:** ALBs can handle SSL/TLS termination, offloading the encryption/decryption process from the application servers, which improves overall system performance.
- **WebSocket and HTTP/2 Support:** ALBs natively support WebSocket and HTTP/2, making them suitable for modern web applications that require these protocols for faster and more efficient communication.
- **Flexible Rules:** ALBs allow users to configure rules that can direct traffic based on HTTP methods, query strings, or request parameters, enabling highly customizable traffic management.

Use Cases:

- Web applications requiring content-based routing, such as e-commerce platforms, SaaS applications, and multi-tenant systems.
- Applications where advanced traffic routing, SSL termination, and protocol support (e.g., HTTP/2, WebSockets) are needed.

Both types of load balancers play essential roles in different scenarios, depending on the specific needs of the application or service.

4. (a) Define a sensor with reference to an IoT device. Explain its characteristics. List and explain any four IoT sensors along with their functions in the IoT devices. 10

Ans: In the context of an Internet of Things (IoT) device, a **sensor** is a hardware component that detects and measures physical properties or environmental conditions and converts these measurements into signals that can be interpreted by the IoT device. These signals are typically sent to a central system or cloud platform for processing, analysis, and action. Sensors are fundamental to IoT devices as they enable the collection of data from the physical world, allowing IoT systems to monitor, analyse, and respond to various conditions or events.

Characteristics of Sensors

1. Sensitivity:

Sensitivity refers to the sensor's ability to detect even small changes in the physical property it is measuring. A highly sensitive sensor can detect minor variations in its environment, making it suitable for applications requiring precise measurements.

2. Accuracy:

Accuracy is the degree to which the sensor's measurements match the true value of the measured property. High accuracy is crucial for applications where precise and reliable data is needed, such as in medical or industrial environments.

3. Range:

The range of a sensor indicates the span of values over which it can measure the physical property. A sensor with a broader range can monitor a wider variety of conditions.

4. Response Time:

Response time is the speed at which a sensor can detect a change in the measured property and provide an output. Fast response times are essential for real-time applications, such as in automotive safety systems or industrial automation.

5. Reliability:

Reliability refers to the sensor's ability to consistently perform its intended function over time without failure. Sensors used in critical applications, like healthcare monitoring, must be highly reliable.

6. Durability:

Durability is the sensor's ability to withstand harsh environmental conditions, such as extreme temperatures, humidity, or mechanical stress. Durable sensors are necessary for outdoor or industrial IoT applications.

7. Power Consumption:

Low power consumption is important for sensors used in battery-powered IoT devices. Energy-efficient sensors help prolong battery life, which is critical for remote or portable applications.

Four IoT Sensors and Their Functions

1. Temperature Sensor

A temperature sensor measures the amount of heat energy or coldness generated by an object or environment. It converts this data into a readable format, such as an electrical signal, which can be processed by an IoT device.

Function in IoT Devices:

- **Smart Homes:** Temperature sensors are used in smart thermostats to monitor indoor temperature and adjust heating or cooling systems automatically.
- **Industrial Automation:** In industrial settings, temperature sensors monitor machinery and equipment to prevent overheating and ensure optimal operating conditions.
- **Healthcare:** Temperature sensors are used in medical devices to monitor body temperature in patients, providing crucial data for health management.

2. Motion Sensor

A motion sensor detects movement within a specific area. It can sense physical movement by detecting changes in the infrared radiation emitted by surrounding objects or by using other methods like ultrasonic or microwave detection.

Function in IoT Devices:

- **Security Systems:** Motion sensors are commonly used in security systems to detect unauthorized movement, triggering alarms or notifications.
- **Smart Lighting:** In smart home systems, motion sensors can automate lighting, turning lights on or off based on the presence of people in a room.
- **Automation:** In industrial environments, motion sensors can be used to monitor and control the movement of machinery, ensuring safety and efficiency.

3. Humidity Sensor

A humidity sensor, also known as a hygrometer, measures the moisture content in the air. It detects the relative humidity and converts it into an electrical signal that can be read by an IoT device.

Function in IoT Devices:

- **Climate Control:** Humidity sensors are used in HVAC (Heating, Ventilation, and Air Conditioning) systems to maintain optimal humidity levels in buildings, improving comfort and air quality.
- **Agriculture:** In precision agriculture, humidity sensors help monitor soil moisture and environmental humidity, enabling better irrigation management and crop health monitoring.
- **Smart Homes:** Humidity sensors in smart homes help control dehumidifiers and air purifiers to maintain a comfortable indoor environment.

4. Proximity Sensor

A proximity sensor detects the presence of an object without physical contact. It emits an electromagnetic field or a beam of radiation (such as infrared) and detects changes in the field or return signal to determine the presence or absence of an object.

Function in IoT Devices:

- **Smartphones:** Proximity sensors in smartphones detect when the phone is close to the user's face during a call, automatically turning off the display to save battery and prevent accidental touches.
- **Automotive Systems:** In vehicles, proximity sensors are used for parking assistance, detecting obstacles near the car and alerting the driver.
- **Industrial Automation:** Proximity sensors are widely used in industrial automation for detecting the position of parts, controlling machinery, and ensuring safety.

These sensors play a vital role in the functioning of IoT devices, making them capable of interacting with and responding to their environments in intelligent ways.

(b) What is cloud security? What are the threats to cloud security? Explain various information security methods is cloud computing. 10

Ans: Cloud Security refers to a set of policies, technologies, and controls designed to protect data, applications, and the associated infrastructure in cloud computing environments. Cloud security ensures that the data stored and processed in the cloud is safe from unauthorized access, data breaches, cyber-attacks, and other threats. It encompasses measures to protect both the cloud provider's infrastructure and the user's data and applications that reside in the cloud.

Cloud security is crucial because cloud environments are often shared by multiple tenants, accessed over the internet, and managed by third-party providers, all of which introduce potential security risks. Effective cloud security must address various aspects, including data confidentiality, integrity, availability, and compliance with legal and regulatory requirements.

Threats to Cloud Security

Several threats can compromise cloud security, including:

1. **Data Breaches:**

Unauthorized access to sensitive data stored in the cloud can lead to data breaches, where personal, financial, or proprietary information is exposed. This can occur due to vulnerabilities in the cloud provider's infrastructure or insufficient security measures on the user's side.

2. Account Hijacking:

Attackers can gain access to cloud user accounts through phishing, credential theft, or exploiting weak authentication mechanisms. Once they have access, they can manipulate or steal data, disrupt services, or use cloud resources for malicious activities.

3. Insider Threats:

Malicious or careless actions by individuals within the organization (e.g., employees, contractors) who have authorized access to the cloud environment can lead to data breaches, unauthorized access, or service disruption.

4. Denial of Service (DoS) Attacks:

DoS attacks aim to overwhelm cloud services with excessive traffic, making them unavailable to legitimate users. This can cause significant downtime, affect business operations, and damage the reputation of the affected organization.

5. Insecure APIs and Interfaces:

Cloud services often expose APIs and interfaces that allow users to manage and interact with cloud resources. If these APIs are not properly secured, attackers can exploit them to gain unauthorized access, manipulate data, or disrupt services.

6. Data Loss:

Data stored in the cloud can be lost due to accidental deletion, hardware failures, or malicious attacks. Without proper backup and recovery strategies, this data loss can be permanent and damaging to the organization.

7. Compliance Violations:

Organizations using cloud services must comply with various regulatory and legal requirements related to data privacy and security. Failure to ensure compliance can result in legal penalties, fines, and loss of customer trust.

Information Security Methods in Cloud Computing

To mitigate these threats, various information security methods can be implemented in cloud computing environments:

1. Data Encryption:

At-Rest Encryption: Encrypts data stored in the cloud to protect it from unauthorized access. Even if attackers gain access to the storage, they cannot read the encrypted data without the appropriate decryption key.

In-Transit Encryption: Ensures that data transmitted between the user's device and the cloud or between cloud services is encrypted. This prevents interception and tampering by attackers during transmission.

End-to-End Encryption: Encrypts data from the source (user) to the destination (cloud) without decryption at intermediate points, ensuring complete protection throughout the data lifecycle.

2. Identity and Access Management (IAM):

Multi-Factor Authentication (MFA): Requires users to provide multiple forms of identification (e.g., password, fingerprint, SMS code) to access cloud resources, significantly reducing the risk of account hijacking.

Role-Based Access Control (RBAC): Assigns permissions based on the user's role within the organization, ensuring that users only have access to the resources they need to perform their jobs.

Access Policies: Implement policies that define who can access what resources, when, and under what conditions, providing fine-grained control over access to cloud resources.

3. Security Monitoring and Threat Detection:

Intrusion Detection and Prevention Systems (IDPS): Monitor cloud environments for signs of malicious activity, such as unauthorized access attempts or suspicious network traffic, and take action to prevent or mitigate attacks.

Security Information and Event Management (SIEM): Collects and analyzes security-related data from cloud resources to identify and respond to potential security threats in real time.

4. Regular Security Audits and Compliance Checks:

Conduct regular security audits to assess the effectiveness of security measures and identify potential vulnerabilities in the cloud environment.

Ensure that cloud services comply with relevant regulatory standards (e.g., GDPR, HIPAA, PCI-DSS) by conducting compliance checks and working with the cloud provider to address any gaps.

5. Data Backup and Disaster Recovery:

Implement robust data backup strategies to ensure that copies of critical data are regularly backed up to a secure location. In the event of data loss, these backups can be used to restore the data quickly.

Develop and test disaster recovery plans that outline the steps to be taken in case of a major security breach or failure, ensuring minimal downtime and data loss.

6. Application Security:
Secure cloud applications by following best practices such as secure coding, regular patching and updating, and vulnerability testing. Ensuring that applications running in the cloud are secure helps prevent exploitation of software vulnerabilities.
7. Zero Trust Security Model:
Adopt a Zero Trust approach, which assumes that no user, device, or application should be trusted by default, even if they are inside the network perimeter. Continuous verification, least privilege access, and strict identity verification are key components of Zero Trust.
8. Shared Responsibility Model:
Understand the shared responsibility model in cloud computing, where the cloud provider is responsible for securing the underlying infrastructure, while the user is responsible for securing their data, applications, and configurations. Both parties must work together to ensure comprehensive security.

By implementing these security methods, organizations can significantly reduce the risks associated with cloud computing and ensure that their data and applications remain secure in the cloud.

5. Write short notes on the following: 4*5=20
(a) Public and private clouds
(b) Challenges in cloud computing
(c) Hierarchical structure of cloud
(d) Use case of edge computing
Ans:
(a) Public and Private Clouds
Public Cloud:
A public cloud is a cloud computing model where cloud services (e.g., storage, compute, networking) are delivered over the internet by third-party providers and are available to the general public. Users share the same infrastructure, which is managed and maintained by the cloud provider.

Features:
- **Scalability:** Public clouds offer virtually unlimited scalability, allowing users to quickly scale resources up or down as needed.
- **Cost-Effectiveness:** Public clouds operate on a pay-as-you-go model, where users pay only for the resources they consume, making it cost-effective for many businesses.
- **Accessibility:** Resources and services in public clouds can be accessed from anywhere with an internet connection.

Examples: Amazon Web Services (AWS), Microsoft Azure, Google Cloud Platform (GCP).

Private Cloud:
A private cloud is a cloud computing model where cloud infrastructure is dedicated to a single organization. It can be hosted on-premises or by a third-party provider, but the resources are not shared with other organizations.

Features:
- **Customization:** Private clouds offer greater customization and control over the infrastructure, allowing organizations to tailor the environment to their specific needs.
- **Security:** Since the infrastructure is dedicated to a single organization, private clouds can offer enhanced security and compliance with industry regulations.
- **Performance:** Private clouds can provide more consistent performance, as resources are not shared with other users.

Examples: VMware vSphere, OpenStack, IBM Private Cloud.

(b) Challenges in Cloud Computing
Security and Privacy:
- Ensuring the security and privacy of data in cloud environments is a significant challenge. Organizations must protect sensitive data from unauthorized access, breaches, and compliance violations, while cloud providers must secure the underlying infrastructure.

Compliance:
- Organizations using cloud services must comply with various regulatory requirements related to data storage, processing, and privacy. Ensuring that cloud environments meet these regulations can be complex, especially in multi-jurisdictional scenarios.

Data Transfer and Bandwidth:
- Moving large volumes of data to and from the cloud can be time-consuming and expensive. Limited bandwidth can lead to slow data transfers, impacting performance and increasing costs.

Vendor Lock-In:
- Once an organization commits to a specific cloud provider, migrating to another provider can be difficult and costly due to differences in platforms, tools, and APIs, leading to vendor lock-in.

Downtime and Reliability:
- Although cloud providers offer high availability, outages and downtime can still occur, potentially disrupting business operations. Organizations must plan for disaster recovery and ensure business continuity.

Cost Management:
- While cloud computing can reduce infrastructure costs, managing and predicting cloud costs can be challenging, especially with variable usage patterns and the complexity of cloud pricing models.

(c) Hierarchical Structure of Cloud
The hierarchical structure of cloud computing is a conceptual model that organizes cloud resources and services into different layers or levels. This structure helps in managing and understanding the various components and services within a cloud environment.

Layers in the Hierarchical Structure:
1. Infrastructure Layer (IaaS):
- The bottom layer consists of the fundamental computing resources, such as virtual machines, storage, and networking. This layer provides the basic infrastructure needed to build and deploy applications. Examples include Amazon EC2, Google Compute Engine, and Microsoft Azure VMs.
2. Platform Layer (PaaS):
- The middle layer provides a platform for developers to build, test, and deploy applications without worrying about the underlying infrastructure. This layer includes development tools, databases, middleware, and runtime environments. Examples include Google App Engine, Microsoft Azure App Services, and Heroku.
3. Application Layer (SaaS):
- The top layer consists of fully functional applications delivered over the internet. Users can access these applications through a web browser without managing the underlying platform or infrastructure. Examples include Google Workspace, Microsoft Office 365, and Salesforce.
Purpose:
- The hierarchical structure helps in organizing cloud services, ensuring that users can select the appropriate level of abstraction based on their needs, whether they require raw infrastructure, a development platform, or complete applications.

(d) Use Case of Edge Computing
Smart Traffic Management:
Scenario:
In a smart city, traffic management systems are deployed to monitor and control traffic flow in real-time. The goal is to reduce congestion, manage traffic signals, and ensure road safety by processing data from various sensors and cameras placed throughout the city.

Working:
- **Data Collection:** Sensors and cameras placed at traffic intersections and along roads collect real-time data on vehicle speed, traffic density, and pedestrian movement.

- **Edge Processing:** Edge computing devices located near these data sources (e.g., at intersections) process the data locally, analysing traffic patterns and predicting congestion. This enables immediate adjustments to traffic signals and provides real-time alerts to drivers via connected vehicles or mobile apps.
- **Real-Time Decision Making:** Based on the processed data, the edge devices can dynamically adjust traffic lights, control pedestrian crossings, and suggest alternative routes to drivers to alleviate congestion.
- **Cloud Interaction:** Aggregated data from multiple edge devices can be sent to the cloud for long-term analysis, such as identifying patterns over time, planning infrastructure improvements, or optimizing traffic management strategies.

Advantages:

- **Low Latency:** Edge computing reduces latency by processing data close to the source, enabling real-time decision-making, which is critical for traffic management.
- **Bandwidth Efficiency:** By processing data locally, edge computing reduces the amount of data sent to the cloud, conserving bandwidth and lowering costs.
- **Improved Safety:** Real-time monitoring and response improve road safety by enabling quick reactions to changing traffic conditions or emergencies.

Edge computing's ability to process data close to the source makes it ideal for applications like smart traffic management, where timely and efficient decision-making is crucial for system effectiveness.

These short notes provide a concise overview of each topic, highlighting the key concepts, challenges, and practical applications related to cloud and edge computing.

Master Of Computer Applications (MCA)
Chapter 4: Term-End Examination, Dec, 2023
MCS-227: Cloud Computing and Iot

Time: 3 Hours
Maximum Marks: 100
Weightage: 70
Note: Question No. 1 is computer. Answer any three Questions from the rest.

1. (a) With reference to the Cloud Architecture, explain the following layers: 10
(i) Client access layer
(ii) Internet connectivity leyer
(iii) Cloud service management layer
(iv) Layer of physical resources

Ans: In cloud computing, the architecture is organized into several layers, each playing a critical role in delivering cloud services. The following are explanations of the key layers in cloud architecture:

(i) Client Access Layer
The Client Access Layer is the topmost layer in the cloud architecture, where end-users interact with cloud services. This layer includes the interfaces and tools that users use to access cloud services, such as web browsers, mobile apps, desktop applications, or APIs. The client access layer ensures that users can easily and securely connect to and utilize cloud resources.

Key Functions:
- **User Interface:** Provides the graphical or command-line interfaces that users interact with to access cloud services.
- **Authentication and Authorization:** Manages user credentials and ensures that only authorized users can access specific cloud services.
- **Session Management:** Handles the creation, maintenance, and termination of user sessions while interacting with cloud services.
- **Device Compatibility:** Ensures that the cloud services can be accessed from various devices (e.g., desktops, laptops, smartphones, tablets).

Examples:
- Web portals for accessing cloud applications (e.g., Google Workspace, Microsoft Office 365).
- Mobile apps for managing cloud services (e.g., AWS Mobile App, Azure App).

(ii) Internet Connectivity Layer
The Internet Connectivity Layer is responsible for connecting the client devices to the cloud services over the internet. This layer includes the network infrastructure, such as routers, switches, firewalls, and ISPs (Internet Service Providers), that enables data transmission between the user's device and the cloud data centers.

Key Functions:
- **Data Transmission:** Facilitates the transmission of data between the user's device and cloud servers over the internet.
- **Network Security:** Implements security measures, such as firewalls, VPNs, and encryption, to protect data during transit and ensure secure communication.
- **Bandwidth Management:** Manages the available bandwidth to ensure efficient and reliable data transfer, especially for high-demand applications.
- **Latency Optimization:** Reduces latency by optimizing network paths and using technologies like Content Delivery Networks (CDNs) to bring content closer to the user.

Examples:
- Internet Service Providers (ISPs) that provide the necessary bandwidth for cloud access.

- Virtual Private Networks (VPNs) that secure data transmission between clients and cloud services.

(iii) Cloud Service Management Layer

The Cloud Service Management Layer is responsible for managing and orchestrating the various cloud services and resources. This layer provides the tools, interfaces, and automation needed to provision, monitor, and maintain cloud services. It plays a critical role in ensuring that cloud services are delivered efficiently and meet the required performance, security, and availability standards.

Key Functions:

- **Provisioning:** Automates the deployment and configuration of cloud resources, such as virtual machines, storage, and networks, based on user requirements.
- **Monitoring:** Continuously monitors the performance, availability, and security of cloud services, ensuring that they operate within predefined thresholds.
- **Resource Allocation:** Manages the allocation of resources to various cloud services, optimizing utilization and cost-efficiency.
- **Service Level Management:** Ensures that cloud services meet the agreed-upon Service Level Agreements (SLAs) by monitoring key performance indicators (KPIs) and taking corrective actions when necessary.
- **Billing and Reporting:** Tracks resource usage and generates billing reports, providing transparency and accountability for cloud service consumption.

Examples:

- AWS Management Console for managing AWS cloud resources.
- Azure Portal for provisioning and monitoring Microsoft Azure services.

(iv) Layer of Physical Resources

The Layer of Physical Resources represents the foundational layer in cloud architecture, comprising the physical infrastructure that powers the cloud. This includes data centers, servers, storage devices, networking hardware, and other physical components that support the virtualization and delivery of cloud services. The physical resources layer is managed by the cloud provider, ensuring that the underlying hardware is reliable, secure, and scalable.

Key Functions:

- **Data Centers:** Facilities that house the physical infrastructure, including servers, storage, and networking equipment, providing the environment necessary for cloud operations.
- **Servers:** Physical machines that host virtual machines, applications, and data storage, forming the backbone of cloud services.
- **Storage:** Physical storage devices (e.g., SSDs, HDDs) that store data for cloud applications and services, ensuring data availability and redundancy.
- **Networking Hardware:** Includes routers, switches, and firewalls that enable communication between physical servers and external networks, ensuring data flow within and outside the data center.
- **Power and Cooling:** Manages power distribution and cooling systems to ensure the continuous operation of data centers, maintaining optimal conditions for hardware performance.

Examples:

- Google's data centers that host the infrastructure for Google Cloud Platform (GCP).
- Amazon's data centers that power AWS services.

Each layer plays a critical role in ensuring the seamless delivery, management, and security of cloud services, making cloud computing a robust and scalable solution for modern IT needs.

(b) What is load-balancing? Why is it imperative in cloud computing to balance the cloud-load? Also, explain briefly hardware-based load balancer and virtual load balancer. 10

Ans: Load Balancing is the process of distributing incoming network traffic or workloads across multiple servers or resources to ensure that no single server or resource is overwhelmed. The primary goal of load balancing is to optimize resource use, maximize throughput, minimize response time, and ensure reliability and availability of services. Load balancers can distribute the load based on various algorithms, such as round-robin, least connections, or weighted distribution, to ensure that traffic is handled efficiently.

Importance of Load Balancing in Cloud Computing

In cloud computing, load balancing is imperative for several reasons:

1. Scalability:

Cloud environments often need to scale dynamically to handle varying amounts of traffic. Load balancing ensures that as the demand increases, the load is distributed across multiple servers or instances, preventing any single server from becoming a bottleneck.

2. High Availability and Reliability:

By distributing traffic across multiple servers, load balancing ensures that if one server fails or becomes unavailable, the load is automatically redirected to other healthy servers. This redundancy enhances the availability and reliability of cloud services.

3. Performance Optimization:

Load balancing optimizes the performance of cloud applications by ensuring that traffic is evenly distributed, preventing server overloads, reducing response times, and improving user experience.

4. Resource Utilization:

Efficient load balancing ensures that resources are utilized optimally, reducing the chances of under-utilization or overloading any particular server. This leads to better cost efficiency in cloud environments.

5. Disaster Recovery:

Load balancers can help in disaster recovery by distributing traffic to different data centers or geographic locations in the event of a failure, ensuring continuity of service.

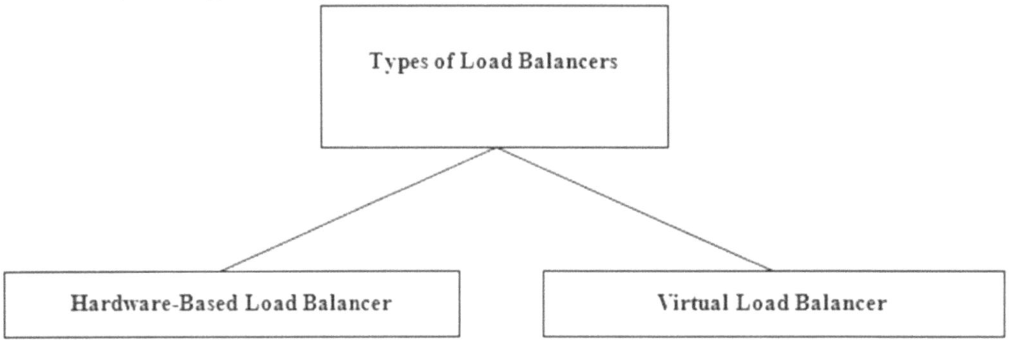

Types of Load Balancers

(i) Hardware-Based Load Balancer

A Hardware-Based Load Balancer is a physical device specifically designed to distribute network traffic across multiple servers. These devices are typically placed at the front of a data center or network to manage and route traffic efficiently. Hardware load balancers are known for their high performance, reliability, and ability to handle large volumes of traffic.

Features:

- **Dedicated Performance:** Hardware load balancers are built with specialized hardware that is optimized for traffic management, offering high throughput and low latency.
- **Advanced Features:** Many hardware load balancers come with advanced features such as SSL offloading, content switching, and application acceleration, which enhance the performance and security of the network.
- **Scalability:** While they offer high performance, hardware load balancers have a fixed capacity, and scaling beyond that capacity requires purchasing additional units, which can be costly.
- **Cost:** Hardware load balancers can be expensive due to the cost of the physical device and associated maintenance and support.

Examples: F5 BIG-IP, Citrix ADC (formerly NetScaler), Cisco ACE.

(ii) Virtual Load Balancer

A Virtual Load Balancer is a software-based solution that performs the same functions as a hardware load balancer but runs on virtualized infrastructure. It can be deployed on a virtual machine, within a cloud environment, or as part of a software-defined networking (SDN) setup. Virtual load balancers offer flexibility, scalability, and cost-effectiveness, making them ideal for cloud environments.

Features:
- **Flexibility:** Virtual load balancers can be easily deployed, configured, and scaled in virtual environments. They can run on commodity hardware, reducing the need for specialized devices.
- **Cost-Effectiveness:** Since virtual load balancers do not require physical hardware, they are generally more cost-effective, particularly for small to medium-sized enterprises or cloud-native applications.
- **Scalability:** Virtual load balancers can scale horizontally by deploying additional instances as traffic increases, providing dynamic scalability in cloud environments.
- **Integration:** They can be seamlessly integrated with cloud platforms, leveraging cloud-native tools and services to enhance their capabilities.

Examples: AWS Elastic Load Balancing (ELB), Microsoft Azure Load Balancer, HAProxy, NGINX Plus.

Both hardware and virtual load balancers play important roles depending on the specific needs of the organization, with hardware load balancers being preferred for high-performance, mission-critical environments, and virtual load balancers offering greater flexibility and cost savings in cloud or virtualized environments.

(c) List and explain any ten emerging IoT technologies. 10

Ans: The Internet of Things (IoT) is continuously evolving, driven by advancements in technology that enhance the capabilities, efficiency, and scalability of IoT solutions. Below are ten emerging IoT technologies that are shaping the future of connected devices:

1. 5G Connectivity

5G is the fifth generation of wireless technology, offering significantly higher speeds, lower latency, and greater capacity compared to previous generations. For IoT, 5G enables faster data transfer and supports a massive number of connected devices, making it ideal for smart cities, autonomous vehicles, and industrial automation.

Impact on IoT:

Enables real-time communication between devices.

Supports large-scale IoT deployments with high data throughput.

2. Edge Computing

Edge Computing involves processing data close to where it is generated, rather than sending it to a centralized cloud for processing. This reduces latency, conserves bandwidth, and allows for real-time decision-making, making it crucial for time-sensitive applications like autonomous vehicles, industrial IoT, and healthcare.

Impact on IoT:

Improves response times and reduces the need for bandwidth.

Enhances data privacy by keeping sensitive data local.

3. Artificial Intelligence (AI) and Machine Learning (ML)

AI and ML are being integrated into IoT systems to enable devices to learn from data, predict outcomes, and make decisions autonomously. These technologies are used in predictive maintenance, smart home systems, and personalized healthcare.

Impact on IoT:

Enables intelligent automation and decision-making.

Improves the efficiency and functionality of IoT systems through data-driven insights.

4. IoT Security Technologies

IoT Security is becoming increasingly important as the number of connected devices grows. Emerging security technologies focus on protecting IoT devices from cyberattacks, ensuring data integrity, and maintaining user privacy. This includes encryption, blockchain for secure transactions, and advanced authentication methods.

Impact on IoT:
Enhances the security of IoT devices and networks.
Protects sensitive data and ensures compliance with regulations.

5. Low-Power Wide-Area Networks (LPWANs)
LPWANs are wireless communication networks designed to cover large areas while using minimal power. Technologies like LoRaWAN, Sigfox, and NB-IoT fall under this category and are ideal for IoT applications that require long-range communication with low power consumption, such as smart agriculture and remote monitoring.

Impact on IoT:
Extends the battery life of IoT devices.
Enables connectivity in remote or rural areas.

6. Blockchain for IoT
Blockchain technology is being applied to IoT to enhance security, transparency, and data integrity. Blockchain can create a decentralized ledger for IoT transactions, making it difficult for malicious actors to tamper with data or devices.

Impact on IoT:
Provides a secure and transparent way to manage IoT data and transactions.
Facilitates decentralized IoT networks, reducing the risk of single points of failure.

7. Digital Twins
Digital Twins are virtual replicas of physical devices or systems. They are used to simulate, monitor, and optimize the performance of IoT devices and systems in real-time. Digital twins are particularly useful in manufacturing, smart cities, and healthcare for predictive maintenance and scenario analysis.

Impact on IoT:
Enhances the monitoring and optimization of IoT systems.
Reduces maintenance costs by predicting failures before they occur.

8. Smart Sensors
Smart Sensors are advanced sensors equipped with data processing and communication capabilities. They not only collect data but also analyse it locally and communicate with other devices. These sensors are used in applications such as environmental monitoring, smart homes, and industrial automation.

Impact on IoT:
Enables real-time data analysis and decision-making at the sensor level.
Reduces the need for constant data transmission, conserving bandwidth.

9. Wearable IoT
Wearable IoT devices are smart gadgets worn on the body, such as smartwatches, fitness trackers, and medical devices. These devices collect data related to health, fitness, and other personal metrics, providing real-time insights and alerts.

Impact on IoT:
Promotes health and wellness through continuous monitoring.
Enables personalized healthcare and proactive medical intervention.

10. Voice-Activated IoT Devices
Voice-Activated IoT Devices are becoming increasingly popular in smart homes and workplaces. These devices use natural language processing (NLP) to understand and respond to voice commands, controlling smart appliances, security systems, and entertainment devices.

Impact on IoT:
Simplifies user interaction with IoT devices through voice commands.

Enhances accessibility for users with disabilities or those who prefer hands-free control.

(d) What is Edge Computing? Explain its working with the help of a use-case. 10

Ans: Edge Computing is a distributed computing paradigm that brings computation and data storage closer to the location where it is needed, typically at or near the source of data generation, such as IoT devices, sensors, or local servers. Instead of relying solely on centralized cloud data centers, edge computing processes data locally, reducing the need to transmit large volumes of data to the cloud. This approach helps to minimize latency, conserve bandwidth, and enable real-time processing and decision-making.

How Edge Computing Works

Edge computing involves deploying computing resources, such as servers, gateways, or embedded systems, at the "edge" of the network,close to the data source. The primary goal is to process data locally to avoid the delays and bandwidth usage associated with sending data to centralized cloud servers for processing.

Steps in Edge Computing:

1. Data Generation:

IoT devices, sensors, or other data-generating equipment produce vast amounts of data in real-time. This data could include temperature readings, video footage, machine vibrations, or any other type of sensor data.

2. Data Transmission:

The generated data is transmitted to nearby edge devices, such as edge servers, gateways, or even powerful embedded systems. This transmission occurs over local networks rather than being sent directly to a cloud data center.

3. Local Processing:

The edge device processes the data locally. This processing can involve filtering, aggregating, analyzing, or applying machine learning models to the data. By processing data at the edge, decisions can be made more quickly, and only relevant data or results are sent to the cloud if necessary.

4. Immediate Actions:

Based on the processed data, the edge device can trigger immediate actions, such as activating an actuator, sending alerts, or adjusting device settings. For example, if an edge device detects a safety issue in an industrial machine, it can shut down the machine instantly to prevent damage.

5. Data Forwarding (Optional):

After processing data locally, the edge device may send a summary, key insights, or relevant data to a central cloud server for further analysis, long-term storage, or reporting. This reduces the amount of data that needs to be sent over the network, conserving bandwidth and reducing costs.

6. User Interaction:

Users can interact with the system through interfaces such as mobile apps, dashboards, or web portals, allowing them to monitor, manage, and control edge devices in real-time.

Use-Case: Smart Traffic Management

In a smart city, traffic management systems are deployed to monitor and control traffic flow in real-time to reduce congestion, manage traffic signals, and ensure road safety. The goal is to process data from various sensors and cameras placed throughout the city, enabling dynamic traffic management based on real-time conditions.

Working:

1. Data Collection:

Sensors and cameras installed at traffic intersections and along roads continuously collect data on vehicle speeds, traffic density, and pedestrian movement. This data is crucial for understanding the real-time traffic situation in different parts of the city.

2. Edge Processing:

Instead of sending all the collected data to a central cloud server, the data is transmitted to edge devices located near the traffic intersections (e.g., edge servers or gateways). These edge devices process the data locally, analysing traffic patterns, detecting congestion, and predicting traffic conditions.

3. Real-Time Decision Making:

Based on the processed data, the edge devices can make real-time decisions to adjust traffic signals, manage pedestrian crossings, and send alerts to drivers about traffic conditions. For example, if an edge device detects that traffic is building up at an intersection, it can adjust the traffic lights to alleviate the congestion.

4. Data Forwarding to the Cloud:

While the edge devices handle real-time processing, they can also send aggregated data or key insights to the central cloud server. The cloud can use this data for long-term analysis, such as identifying traffic trends, planning infrastructure improvements, or optimizing traffic management strategies.

5. User Interaction:

City traffic managers and residents can access real-time traffic information through a mobile app or web dashboard. They can view traffic conditions, receive alerts, and make informed decisions about their travel routes.

Benefits of Edge Computing in this Use-Case:

- **Low Latency:** By processing data locally, edge computing reduces latency, enabling real-time adjustments to traffic signals and other control systems.
- **Bandwidth Efficiency:** Edge computing reduces the need to send large amounts of raw data to the cloud, conserving bandwidth and lowering costs.
- **Improved Safety:** Real-time data processing enhances road safety by enabling quick reactions to changing traffic conditions or emergencies.

This approach enhances the responsiveness and efficiency of IoT applications, particularly in scenarios where real-time processing is critical.

2. (a) Explain the following IoT-connectivity technologies: 10

(i) Zigbee
(ii) Z-wave
(iii) RFID
(iv) NFC

Ans: The following are some of the key connectivity technologies used in IoT (Internet of Things) systems, each with its own unique features and use cases:

(i) Zigbee

Zigbee is a low-power, low-data-rate wireless communication protocol designed for short-range communication. It operates on the IEEE 802.15.4 standard and is widely used in IoT applications that require reliable, low-cost, and energy-efficient communication.

Key Features:

- **Mesh Networking:** Zigbee supports mesh networking, where devices can relay data to one another, extending the communication range and improving network reliability.
- **Low Power Consumption:** Zigbee is designed for low-power operation, making it ideal for battery-powered devices.
- **Short Range:** Zigbee operates over short distances, typically up to 100 meters in indoor environments, making it suitable for home automation and industrial monitoring.
- **Data Rate:** Zigbee typically supports data rates up to 250 kbps, which is sufficient for many IoT applications like smart lighting and temperature control.

Use Cases:

- **Home Automation:** Smart lighting, security systems, and energy management.
- **Industrial Monitoring:** Sensor networks for monitoring equipment and environmental conditions.
- **Healthcare:** Medical devices for remote patient monitoring.

(ii) Z-Wave

Z-Wave is another wireless communication protocol designed for low-power, low-bandwidth applications, particularly in smart home and building automation systems. It operates on a sub-GHz frequency, which helps reduce interference with other wireless networks.

Key Features:

- **Mesh Networking:** Like Zigbee, Z-Wave also supports mesh networking, enabling devices to communicate with each other and route data efficiently across the network.
- **Low Power:** Z-Wave is designed for low power consumption, making it suitable for battery-operated devices.
- **Longer Range:** Z-Wave typically offers a longer range compared to Zigbee, with effective communication distances up to 100 meters indoors and up to 300 meters outdoors, depending on the environment.

- **Interoperability:** Z-Wave has strong interoperability standards, ensuring that devices from different manufacturers can work together seamlessly.

Use Cases:
- **Smart Home:** Control of lights, thermostats, door locks, and security systems.
- **Building Automation:** Energy management and remote control of HVAC systems.
- **Security:** Wireless alarm systems and smart locks.

(iii) RFID (Radio Frequency Identification)
RFID is a wireless communication technology that uses electromagnetic fields to automatically identify and track tags attached to objects. An RFID system typically consists of an RFID reader and RFID tags, which can be passive (no internal power source) or active (powered by a battery).

Key Features:
- **Automatic Identification:** RFID enables the automatic identification and tracking of objects without the need for direct line-of-sight, making it highly efficient for inventory management and asset tracking.
- **Passive and Active Tags:** Passive RFID tags rely on the reader's signal for power, while active RFID tags have their own power source, allowing them to transmit signals over longer distances.
- **Short to Long Range:** RFID systems can operate over varying ranges, from a few centimeters for passive tags to several meters for active tags.
- **Low Data Rate:** RFID typically has low data rates, which is sufficient for the basic identification and tracking information it is used to transmit.

Use Cases:
- **Inventory Management:** Tracking goods in warehouses and retail environments.
- **Asset Tracking:** Monitoring the location and status of equipment and tools in industrial settings.
- **Access Control:** Controlling entry to secure areas using RFID-enabled ID cards.

(iv) NFC (Near Field Communication)
NFC is a short-range wireless communication technology that enables data exchange between devices over a distance of a few centimeters. NFC is based on RFID technology and is commonly used for secure, contactless transactions and data exchange.

Key Features:
- **Very Short Range:** NFC operates over a very short range, typically within 4-10 centimeters, which enhances security by requiring close proximity for communication.
- **Low Power Consumption:** NFC is designed for low power consumption, making it suitable for use in mobile devices and wearables.
- **Ease of Use:** NFC enables quick and easy pairing of devices, making it ideal for applications like mobile payments and data sharing.
- **Two-Way Communication:** Unlike RFID, which is primarily one-way, NFC supports two-way communication, allowing devices to both send and receive data.

Use Cases:
- **Mobile Payments:** Contactless payments using smartphones or NFC-enabled cards (e.g., Apple Pay, Google Pay).
- **Access Control:** Secure entry systems using NFC-enabled cards or smartphones.
- **Data Sharing:** Simple pairing of devices, such as Bluetooth devices or file sharing between smartphones.

These IoT connectivity technologies play crucial roles in enabling various IoT applications by providing the necessary communication channels for devices to interact, share data, and perform their intended functions efficiently and securely.

(b) With reference to cloud-security, explain the following: 10
(i) Identity management
(ii) Access control mechanism

Ans: Cloud security is a critical aspect of cloud computing, ensuring that data, applications, and infrastructure are protected from unauthorized access, breaches, and other security threats. Two fundamental components of cloud security are identity management and access control mechanisms.

(i) Identity Management

Identity Management (IdM) is a framework of policies and technologies used to ensure that the right individuals have access to the right resources within an organization at the right times. In the context of cloud computing, identity management is crucial for managing user identities and controlling access to cloud resources.

Key Functions:

- **Authentication:** Identity management systems authenticate users by verifying their credentials, such as passwords, biometrics, or multi-factor authentication (MFA). This ensures that only legitimate users can access cloud services.
- **User Provisioning and Deprovisioning:** Identity management handles the creation, management, and deletion of user accounts across cloud services. It ensures that new users are provisioned with the necessary access rights and that former employees or unauthorized users are promptly deprovisioned.
- **Single Sign-On (SSO):** SSO allows users to log in once and gain access to multiple cloud services without needing to re-enter credentials for each service. This simplifies the user experience and enhances security by reducing password fatigue.
- **Directory Services Integration:** Identity management systems often integrate with directory services like Active Directory (AD) or Lightweight Directory Access Protocol (LDAP) to manage user identities across cloud and on-premises environments.
- **Federation:** Federated identity management allows users to access cloud resources across multiple organizations or domains using a single set of credentials. This is particularly useful for collaboration between partners or subsidiaries.

Importance in Cloud Security:

- **Centralized Control:** Identity management centralizes the control of user identities, making it easier to enforce security policies and monitor access across all cloud services.
- **Reduced Risk of Unauthorized Access:** By ensuring that only authenticated and authorized users can access cloud resources, identity management helps mitigate the risk of data breaches and unauthorized access.
- **Compliance:** Effective identity management helps organizations meet regulatory requirements related to data access and security, such as GDPR, HIPAA, or PCI-DSS.

(ii) Access Control Mechanism

Access Control Mechanisms are the processes and technologies used to regulate who can access specific resources in a cloud environment and what actions they can perform. Access control is a critical component of cloud security, ensuring that only authorized users can interact with sensitive data and resources.

Key Types of Access Control:

- **Role-Based Access Control (RBAC):**

Explanation: RBAC assigns access rights based on the roles within an organization. Each role is associated with specific permissions, and users are granted roles according to their job responsibilities. This simplifies the management of access rights by grouping permissions by role rather than by individual user.

Example: In a cloud-based financial application, an "Accountant" role might have access to view and edit financial records, while a "Manager" role might have additional permissions to approve transactions.

- **Attribute-Based Access Control (ABAC):**

Explanation: ABAC grants access based on attributes of the user, resource, or environment, such as the user's department, location, or the sensitivity of the data. ABAC provides a more fine-grained access control mechanism than RBAC by considering multiple factors when making access decisions.

Example: A cloud system may grant access to certain data only if the user is from the "Finance" department, is located within the corporate network, and is accessing the data during business hours.

- **Discretionary Access Control (DAC):**

Explanation: In DAC, the owner of a resource (e.g., file or application) has the discretion to decide who can access it and what they can do with it. This type of access control is flexible but can be harder to manage in larger organizations.

Example: In a cloud file storage service, a user might share a document with specific colleagues and decide whether they can view, edit, or share the document with others.

- Mandatory Access Control (MAC):
Explanation: MAC enforces strict access control policies based on predefined rules, typically set by a central authority. Users cannot change access rights. MAC is often used in environments that require high security, such as government or military applications.
Example: In a cloud system with MAC, access to classified information would be controlled strictly based on security clearances, with no ability for users to alter access rights.

Importance in Cloud Security:
- **Protection of Sensitive Data:** Access control mechanisms ensure that only authorized users can access sensitive data and resources, reducing the risk of data breaches.
- **Minimized Insider Threats:** By restricting access based on roles, attributes, or strict rules, organizations can minimize the risk posed by insider threats, where users might misuse their access to sensitive information.
- **Compliance and Auditability:** Access control mechanisms support compliance with regulatory requirements by providing detailed logs of who accessed what resources and when. This auditability is crucial for demonstrating compliance with data protection regulations.

Both identity management and access control are essential components of cloud security, working together to ensure that only the right users have access to the right resources, thereby protecting the organization's data and infrastructure from unauthorized access and breaches.

3. (a) Explain any five applications of cloud computing. 5
Ans: Cloud computing has revolutionized the way organizations and individuals manage, process, and store data, offering a wide range of applications across various industries. Here are five key applications of cloud computing:

1. Data Storage and Backup
One of the most common applications of cloud computing is data storage. Cloud storage services allow individuals and organizations to store and back up their data on remote servers, which can be accessed from anywhere with an internet connection. This eliminates the need for physical storage devices and provides a scalable, secure, and cost-effective solution for managing data.

Examples:
- **Google Drive:** A cloud storage service that allows users to store files and access them from any device.
- **Dropbox:** A popular cloud storage platform for individuals and businesses to store, share, and collaborate on files.

Benefits:
- **Scalability:** Easily increase storage capacity as needed without investing in additional hardware.
- **Data Protection:** Automated backups and redundancy ensure data is protected against loss or corruption.
- **Accessibility:** Access data from any device, anywhere, anytime.

2. Software as a Service (SaaS)
Cloud computing enables the delivery of software applications over the internet through the Software as a Service (SaaS) model. Users can access and use software applications hosted in the cloud without the need to install or maintain the software on their local devices. SaaS is commonly used for applications like email, customer relationship management (CRM), and office productivity suites.

Examples:
- **Microsoft Office 365:** A cloud-based suite of productivity tools, including Word, Excel, and PowerPoint, that can be accessed from any device.
- **Salesforce:** A leading CRM platform that helps businesses manage customer relationships, sales, and marketing activities.

Benefits:
- **Cost-Efficiency:** Reduces the need for upfront software purchases and maintenance, as users typically pay on a subscription basis.
- **Automatic Updates:** Software is automatically updated by the provider, ensuring users always have access to the latest features and security patches.

- **Flexibility:** Users can access the software from any device with an internet connection.

3. Disaster Recovery and Business Continuity
Cloud computing plays a crucial role in disaster recovery and business continuity planning. By storing data and applications in the cloud, organizations can ensure that they remain accessible even in the event of a disaster, such as a hardware failure, natural disaster, or cyberattack. Cloud-based disaster recovery solutions allow for quick data restoration and minimize downtime.

Examples:
AWS Disaster Recovery: Amazon Web Services offers disaster recovery solutions that enable businesses to quickly recover their IT infrastructure and data after a disruption.
Azure Site Recovery: Microsoft Azure provides disaster recovery services to keep applications running during outages by replicating workloads to a secondary location.

Benefits:
Reduced Downtime: Quick data recovery and system restoration minimize business disruption during a disaster.
Cost Savings: Cloud-based disaster recovery is more cost-effective than traditional on-premises solutions, as it eliminates the need for redundant physical infrastructure.
Scalability: Easily scale disaster recovery resources up or down based on business needs.

4. Big Data Analytics
Cloud computing provides the necessary infrastructure and tools to process and analyse vast amounts of data, known as Big Data. Organizations can use cloud-based analytics platforms to gain insights from their data, which can be used for decision-making, improving customer experiences, and optimizing operations. Cloud computing allows businesses to handle the scale and complexity of Big Data without investing in expensive on-premises infrastructure.

Examples:
Google BigQuery: A fully managed data warehouse that enables businesses to analyse large datasets quickly and efficiently using SQL.
AWS Redshift: Amazon's cloud-based data warehousing service that allows organizations to run complex queries on petabytes of structured and semi-structured data.

Benefits:
Scalability: Handle large volumes of data with the ability to scale resources on demand.
Cost-Efficiency: Pay for the computing power and storage used, avoiding the need for large upfront investments in hardware.
Advanced Analytics: Access to powerful analytics tools and machine learning capabilities in the cloud.

5. Cloud-Based Development and Testing
Cloud computing provides an ideal environment for software development and testing. Development teams can use cloud-based platforms to create, test, and deploy applications without the need for physical infrastructure. These platforms offer tools for continuous integration and continuous deployment (CI/CD), enabling faster and more efficient development cycles.

Examples:
AWS Elastic Beanstalk: A cloud service that allows developers to deploy and manage applications quickly without worrying about the underlying infrastructure.
Microsoft Azure DevOps: A set of development tools and services in the cloud that support the entire software development lifecycle, from planning to code management and deployment.

Benefits:
Flexibility: Easily create and manage development environments in the cloud, adapting to the needs of different projects.
Collaboration: Teams can collaborate in real-time using cloud-based tools, regardless of their physical location.
Efficiency: Accelerate the development process with automated testing, deployment, and scaling of applications.

These applications demonstrate the versatility and impact of cloud computing across various domains, enhancing efficiency, scalability, and innovation for businesses and individuals alike.

(b) Write a short note on utility computing. 5

Ans: Utility Computing is a model of computing in which computing resources, such as processing power, storage, and network bandwidth, are provided to users on demand, similar to a utility service like electricity or water. In this model, users can access and pay for computing resources based on their actual usage rather than owning and maintaining their own infrastructure. The term "utility" reflects the idea that these resources are available as needed, with the ability to scale up or down based on the user's requirements.

Key Characteristics of Utility Computing:

1. On-Demand Resource Availability:

Users can access computing resources whenever they need them, without having to invest in or manage physical infrastructure. This allows for greater flexibility and agility, especially for businesses that have variable or unpredictable workloads.

2. Pay-as-You-Go Pricing:

Utility computing typically follows a pay-as-you-go pricing model, where users are billed based on their actual consumption of resources. This cost model is similar to how utilities like electricity are billed, making it a cost-effective option for businesses that want to avoid large upfront capital expenditures.

3. Scalability:

Utility computing allows for easy scalability, meaning users can quickly increase or decrease their resource consumption based on their needs. This is particularly beneficial for businesses that experience seasonal spikes in demand or sudden increases in workload.

4. Managed Services:

The service provider manages the underlying infrastructure, including hardware maintenance, software updates, and security. This allows users to focus on their core business activities without worrying about the complexities of managing IT resources.

5. Resource Pooling:

Resources in a utility computing environment are pooled together and shared among multiple users. This resource pooling enables efficient utilization of resources and often leads to cost savings for users.

Examples of Utility Computing:

- **Cloud Computing Platforms:** Services like Amazon Web Services (AWS), Microsoft Azure, and Google Cloud Platform provide utility computing by offering on-demand access to virtual machines, storage, databases, and other IT resources.
- **Grid Computing:** In grid computing, resources are pooled together from multiple locations to handle large-scale tasks, such as scientific computations, on an as-needed basis.
- **Infrastructure as a Service (IaaS):** IaaS is a form of utility computing where users rent virtualized infrastructure, such as servers and storage, from a cloud provider and pay based on usage.

Benefits of Utility Computing:

- **Cost Efficiency:** By paying only for what they use, organizations can reduce their IT costs and avoid the financial burden of maintaining underutilized hardware.
- **Flexibility:** Utility computing provides the flexibility to adapt to changing business needs without the constraints of fixed infrastructure.
- **Resource Optimization:** The pooling and shared usage of resources lead to better optimization, reducing waste and improving overall efficiency.
- **Focus on Core Business:** With the service provider managing the infrastructure, businesses can focus more on their core operations rather than IT management.

(c) Explain the evolution of cloud computing. 5

Ans: Cloud computing, as we know it today, is the result of decades of technological advancements in computing, networking, and data storage. Its evolution is marked by several key milestones, each contributing to the development of the cloud services that are now integral to modern IT infrastructure.

Here's a look at the evolution of cloud computing:

1. Mainframe Computing (1950s - 1970s)

Early Beginnings:

The roots of cloud computing can be traced back to the era of mainframe computing in the 1950s and 1960s. Mainframes were large, powerful computers used by businesses and governments for centralized data processing. Users accessed these systems through "dumb terminals" that provided no computing power themselves but allowed multiple users to interact with the mainframe.

This concept of centralized computing resources accessible to multiple users laid the foundation for the idea of cloud computing.

2. Time-Sharing and Virtualization (1960s - 1970s)

Time-Sharing:

In the 1960s, the concept of time-sharing emerged, which allowed multiple users to share computing resources simultaneously. This was a significant step towards the multi-user environments that cloud computing relies on today.

Virtualization:

The development of virtualization technology in the 1970s by IBM allowed for the creation of multiple virtual machines (VMs) on a single physical machine. Virtualization made it possible to optimize the use of computing resources and is a core technology in cloud computing, enabling the efficient sharing of physical infrastructure.

3. Client-Server Architecture (1980s - 1990s)

Distributed Computing:

The 1980s and 1990s saw the rise of client-server architecture, where computing tasks were distributed between servers (which provided resources and services) and clients (which requested services). This architecture decentralized computing, making it more scalable and flexible, a precursor to modern cloud services.

Internet and Web Development:

The growth of the internet in the 1990s and the development of web technologies like HTML and HTTP enabled the creation of online services accessible from anywhere. This era laid the groundwork for web-based applications, a key component of cloud computing.

4. Grid Computing and Utility Computing (1990s - Early 2000s)

Grid Computing:

In the late 1990s, the concept of grid computing emerged, allowing geographically dispersed computing resources to work together on complex tasks. Grid computing focused on harnessing the power of many computers to solve large-scale problems, similar to the distributed nature of cloud computing.

Utility Computing:

Around the same time, utility computing began to gain traction. This model proposed that computing resources should be provided on a pay-as-you-go basis, much like utilities such as electricity or water. The idea of utility computing directly influenced the development of cloud computing's pay-per-use model.

5. The Emergence of Cloud Computing (2000s)

Early Cloud Services:

The early 2000s marked the beginning of cloud computing as we know it today. Companies like Amazon, Google, and Salesforce started offering cloud-based services. In 2002, Amazon launched Amazon Web Services (AWS), initially offering simple storage services and computing power, which eventually evolved into a comprehensive cloud platform.

Software as a Service (SaaS):

Salesforce, founded in 1999, pioneered the Software as a Service (SaaS) model by delivering CRM software over the internet. SaaS became one of the most popular models for delivering software, reducing the need for on-premises installations and maintenance.

6. Growth and Expansion (2010s - Present)

Widespread Adoption:

By the 2010s, cloud computing had become mainstream, with businesses of all sizes adopting cloud services for a wide range of applications, from data storage and processing to software development and analytics.

Introduction of Platform as a Service (PaaS) and Infrastructure as a Service (IaaS):

In addition to SaaS, cloud computing evolved to include Platform as a Service (PaaS) and Infrastructure as a Service (IaaS). PaaS provides a platform for developers to build and deploy applications without worrying about underlying infrastructure, while IaaS offers virtualized computing resources over the internet.

Hybrid and Multi-Cloud Environments:

The 2010s also saw the rise of hybrid and multi-cloud environments, where organizations use a combination of private and public clouds, or multiple cloud providers, to meet their specific needs. This approach offers greater flexibility, scalability, and resilience.

Edge Computing and Serverless Architecture:
More recent developments include edge computing, which brings computation closer to the data source, and serverless architecture, which allows developers to run code without provisioning or managing servers. These advancements are further pushing the boundaries of cloud computing capabilities.

7. Future of Cloud Computing

AI and Machine Learning Integration:
The integration of artificial intelligence (AI) and machine learning (ML) into cloud platforms is becoming increasingly common. Cloud providers are offering AI and ML services that enable businesses to leverage these technologies without the need for specialized infrastructure.

Quantum Computing:
The future of cloud computing may also include quantum computing, which promises to solve complex problems beyond the capabilities of classical computers. Major cloud providers are already experimenting with quantum computing services.

Sustainability and Green Cloud Computing:
As concerns about environmental impact grow, there is a push towards more sustainable cloud computing practices. This includes optimizing data centers for energy efficiency and adopting renewable energy sources to power cloud infrastructure.

(d) Describe briefly the Hybrid-Cloud Deployment Model. 5

Ans: The **Hybrid-Cloud Deployment Model** is a cloud computing environment that combines the use of both private and public cloud infrastructures. In a hybrid cloud, data and applications can move between the private and public clouds, allowing for greater flexibility and more optimized IT solutions.

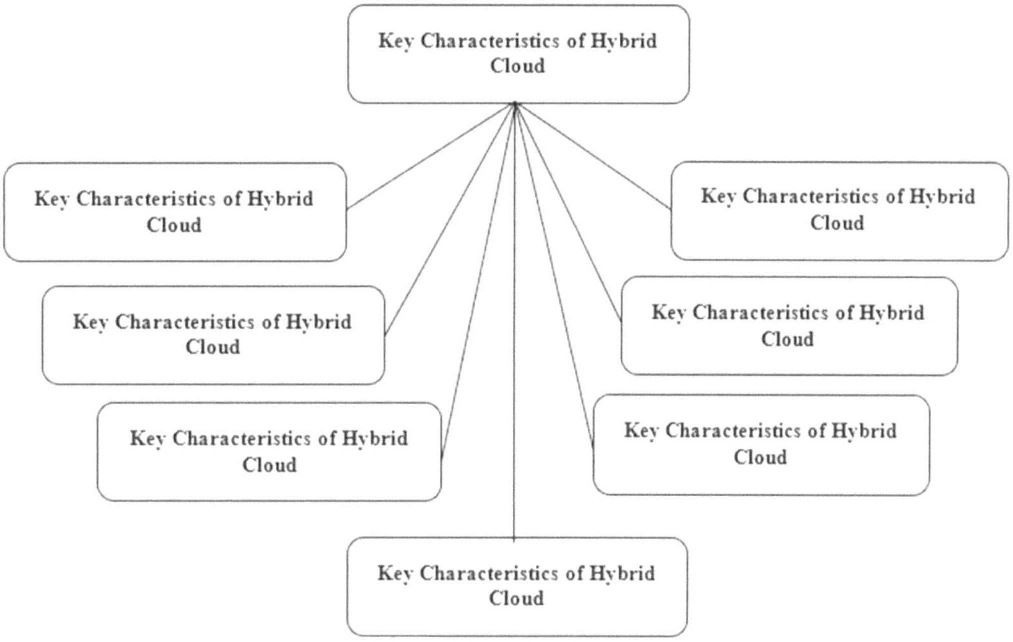

Key Characteristics of Hybrid Cloud:

1. Combination of Public and Private Clouds:
A hybrid cloud environment integrates a private cloud (on-premises or dedicated) with a public cloud (such as AWS, Azure, or Google Cloud). This combination allows organizations to manage some of their resources in-house while taking advantage of the scalability and cost-efficiency of the public cloud.

2. Workload Distribution:
In a hybrid cloud model, workloads can be distributed between the private and public clouds based on specific needs. For example, sensitive data can be stored and processed in the private cloud, while less sensitive workloads can be handled by the public cloud to save costs.

3. Scalability and Flexibility:

Hybrid clouds provide the scalability of public clouds while retaining the control and security of private clouds. Organizations can scale resources up or down in the public cloud as needed, without having to over-provision their private cloud infrastructure.

4. Seamless Integration:

A key feature of hybrid cloud is the seamless integration between private and public clouds. This integration allows data and applications to move freely between environments, providing a unified computing experience.

5. Cost Efficiency:

By using a hybrid cloud model, organizations can optimize costs by keeping predictable, stable workloads in the private cloud and offloading variable, high-demand workloads to the public cloud. This reduces the need for expensive, high-capacity private infrastructure.

Use Cases for Hybrid Cloud:

Data Security and Compliance:

Organizations with strict data security and compliance requirements can store sensitive data in a private cloud while using the public cloud for non-sensitive operations, ensuring that they meet regulatory standards while still benefiting from cloud scalability.

Disaster Recovery and Business Continuity:

Hybrid clouds are ideal for disaster recovery, where critical data and applications are replicated in the public cloud. In the event of a failure in the private cloud, operations can continue with minimal disruption using the public cloud.

Development and Testing:

Development and testing environments can be hosted in the public cloud to take advantage of its scalability and pay-as-you-go model, while production workloads remain in the private cloud for better control and security.

Bursting Workloads:

During peak times, such as during a seasonal sales period, an organization can "burst" additional workloads to the public cloud to handle the increased demand without needing to invest in additional private cloud infrastructure.

Advantages of Hybrid Cloud:

- **Flexibility:** Allows organizations to choose the optimal cloud environment for each workload, balancing performance, security, and cost.
- **Cost Management:** Reduces capital expenditure by utilizing the public cloud for fluctuating or temporary workloads while maintaining critical workloads in a secure private cloud.
- **Enhanced Security:** Sensitive data can be kept within a private cloud, reducing exposure to potential security threats.
- **Improved Disaster Recovery:** Offers robust disaster recovery solutions by leveraging both private and public clouds to ensure business continuity.

Challenges of Hybrid Cloud:

- **Complexity:** Managing a hybrid cloud environment can be complex, requiring robust integration, monitoring, and management tools.
- **Security Risks:** Ensuring consistent security policies and practices across both private and public clouds can be challenging.
- **Data Transfer and Bandwidth:** Moving large amounts of data between private and public clouds can lead to bandwidth issues and potential latency.

4. (a) What is machine or server level virtualization? Briefly explain the following types of server level virtualization: 10

(i) Hypervisor

(ii) Full-virtualization

Ans: Machine or Server-Level Virtualization is a technology that allows multiple virtual machines (VMs) to run on a single physical server. Each virtual machine operates independently, with its own operating system and applications, as if it were running on a separate physical machine. Server-level virtualization abstracts the physical hardware, allowing for more efficient use of resources, improved scalability, and easier management of computing environments.

Server-level virtualization is fundamental to cloud computing, enabling cloud providers to offer Infrastructure as a Service (IaaS), where users can rent virtualized computing resources on demand. This technology is also widely used in data centers to consolidate workloads, reduce hardware costs, and increase flexibility in resource allocation.

Types of Server-Level Virtualization

(i) Hypervisor

A **Hypervisor**, also known as a Virtual Machine Monitor (VMM), is a software layer that sits between the physical hardware and the virtual machines. It is responsible for creating, managing, and running VMs on a host system. The hypervisor allocates physical resources such as CPU, memory, storage, and network bandwidth to each virtual machine, ensuring that they operate independently of each other.

Types of Hypervisors:

Type 1 Hypervisor (Bare-Metal Hypervisor):

This type of hypervisor runs directly on the physical hardware of the server, without the need for a host operating system. It has direct access to the hardware, which allows for better performance and efficiency.

Examples: VMware ESXi, Microsoft Hyper-V, Xen.

Type 2 Hypervisor (Hosted Hypervisor):

This type of hypervisor runs on top of a host operating system. It relies on the host OS for hardware management and provides a virtualized environment for running VMs.

Examples: VMware Workstation, Oracle VirtualBox, Parallels Desktop.

Functions of a Hypervisor:

- **Resource Management:** The hypervisor allocates physical resources to VMs and manages resource contention to ensure optimal performance.
- **Isolation:** It ensures that each VM operates independently and securely, preventing one VM from affecting others.

VM Lifecycle Management: The hypervisor handles the creation, deletion, suspension, and migration of VMs.

- **Hardware Abstraction:** It abstracts the underlying physical hardware, presenting virtualized hardware to each VM.

Importance in Virtualization:

- The hypervisor is the core component of server-level virtualization, enabling multiple VMs to coexist on a single physical server. It is essential for the efficient use of resources and the flexibility of cloud environments.

(ii) Full Virtualization

Full Virtualization is a type of server-level virtualization where the hypervisor provides a complete simulation of the underlying physical hardware, allowing unmodified guest operating systems to run in isolation. In full virtualization, each virtual machine has its own complete set of virtual hardware, including CPU, memory, storage, and network interfaces.

How It Works:

- The hypervisor intercepts and translates all instructions between the guest operating system and the physical hardware. It ensures that the guest OS believes it is running on actual physical hardware, even though it is operating in a virtual environment.
- This type of virtualization does not require any modifications to the guest OS, making it highly compatible with a wide range of operating systems.

Benefits of Full Virtualization:

- **Compatibility:** Since full virtualization does not require any changes to the guest OS, it can run a wide variety of operating systems, including those not designed for virtualization.
- **Isolation:** Each VM is completely isolated from others, ensuring that issues in one VM do not affect the others.
- **Ease of Use:** Full virtualization simplifies the management of VMs because the guest OS can be installed and run as it would on a physical machine.

Challenges of Full Virtualization:

- **Performance Overhead:** Because the hypervisor must translate all interactions between the guest OS and the hardware, there can be a performance overhead compared to other virtualization methods.
- **Complexity:** Full virtualization requires more complex hypervisor software to manage the complete simulation of hardware.

Examples:

VMware ESXi and Microsoft Hyper-V provide full virtualization capabilities, allowing multiple VMs to run unmodified operating systems with complete hardware abstraction.

Both hypervisors and full virtualization are key technologies that make server-level virtualization possible, enabling the efficient and flexible management of computing resources in both traditional data centers and cloud environments.

(b) Explain the following sensors used in 10T devices along with its features and applications: 10
(i) Image sensors
(ii) Chemical sensors
(iii) Acceleration sensors
(iv) Proximity sensors

Ans: Sensors play a crucial role in the functionality of IoT (Internet of Things) devices, enabling them to interact with the physical world by collecting data from their environment. Below are explanations of four types of sensors commonly used in IoT devices, along with their features and applications:

(i) Image Sensors

Image Sensors are electronic devices that convert light into electronic signals. These sensors capture visual information by detecting the intensity, color, and composition of light, which is then processed to create images or video. They are essential components in cameras, smartphones, and various IoT devices that require visual data.

Features:
- **High Resolution:** Image sensors come in various resolutions, with high-resolution sensors providing detailed images, which is crucial for applications like surveillance and medical imaging.
- **Color Detection:** Many image sensors can detect color information, which is important for applications requiring detailed visual analysis.
- **Low Light Performance:** Advanced image sensors are capable of capturing images in low-light conditions, making them useful for night vision and surveillance.

Applications:
- **Smart Surveillance:** Image sensors are used in security cameras to monitor environments, detect intrusions, and provide real-time video feeds.
- **Automotive Systems:** In vehicles, image sensors are used in advanced driver-assistance systems (ADAS) for tasks like lane detection, parking assistance, and collision avoidance.
- **Healthcare:** Medical imaging devices use image sensors for diagnostic purposes, such as in digital X-rays, MRIs, and endoscopes.
- **Smartphones:** Image sensors in smartphones enable photography, video recording, and facial recognition features.

(ii) Chemical Sensors

Chemical Sensors are devices that detect and measure the concentration of specific chemicals or gases in the environment. They work by producing a signal proportional to the chemical's presence, which can then be processed and analysed. These sensors are essential for monitoring air quality, detecting hazardous gases, and controlling chemical processes.

Features:
- **Selectivity:** Chemical sensors can be designed to detect specific chemicals or gases, ensuring accurate measurements even in complex environments.
- **Sensitivity:** They are highly sensitive, capable of detecting low concentrations of chemicals, which is vital for applications like environmental monitoring.
- **Real-Time Monitoring:** Many chemical sensors provide real-time data, allowing for immediate detection and response to hazardous conditions.

Applications:
- **Environmental Monitoring:** Chemical sensors are used to monitor air and water quality by detecting pollutants like carbon monoxide, sulfur dioxide, and nitrogen oxides.

- **Industrial Safety:** In industrial settings, chemical sensors detect toxic or flammable gases to prevent accidents and ensure worker safety.
- **Healthcare:** Breath analysis devices use chemical sensors to detect biomarkers for diseases, such as alcohol levels or glucose in breath.
- **Smart Homes:** Chemical sensors are integrated into smart home systems to detect gas leaks, such as natural gas or carbon monoxide, and trigger alarms.

(iii) Acceleration Sensors

Acceleration Sensors, also known as accelerometers, measure the rate of change in velocity (acceleration) of an object. They can detect both linear and rotational motion and are commonly used in devices to monitor movement, orientation, and vibration.

Features:

- **Multi-Axis Measurement:** Acceleration sensors can measure acceleration along multiple axes (e.g., x, y, z), providing comprehensive data on motion and orientation.
- **High Sensitivity:** They are sensitive enough to detect even small movements, making them suitable for applications requiring precise motion detection.
- **Low Power Consumption:** Many acceleration sensors are designed to consume minimal power, which is important for battery-powered IoT devices.

Applications:

- **Wearable Devices:** Acceleration sensors in fitness trackers and smartwatches monitor physical activity, such as steps taken, calories burned, and sleep patterns.
- **Automotive Systems:** In vehicles, acceleration sensors are used in airbag deployment systems to detect collisions and in stability control systems to monitor vehicle dynamics.
- **Mobile Devices:** Smartphones and tablets use acceleration sensors to detect screen orientation, control gaming inputs, and enable gesture-based commands.
- **Industrial Automation:** In manufacturing, acceleration sensors monitor machinery for vibrations or deviations that could indicate maintenance needs.

(iv) Proximity Sensors

Proximity Sensors detect the presence or absence of an object within a certain range without physical contact. These sensors work by emitting an electromagnetic field or infrared light and measuring the changes in the field or reflected signal to determine the proximity of an object.

Features:

- **Contactless Detection:** Proximity sensors operate without physical contact, reducing wear and tear and enabling detection in harsh environments.
- **Versatility:** They can detect a wide range of materials, including metals, plastics, and glass, making them suitable for diverse applications.
- **Short to Medium Range:** Proximity sensors typically operate over short to medium ranges, making them ideal for detecting objects within close proximity.

Applications:

- **Smartphones:** Proximity sensors in smartphones detect when the device is held close to the ear, turning off the display to prevent accidental touches during a call.
- **Automotive Systems:** In vehicles, proximity sensors are used in parking assistance systems to detect obstacles and provide alerts to the driver.
- **Industrial Automation:** Proximity sensors are used to detect the position of objects on production lines, ensuring proper alignment and quality control.
- **Security Systems:** Proximity sensors are used in access control systems to detect the presence of authorized personnel or to trigger alarms when unauthorized access is attempted.

These sensors are fundamental components of IoT devices, enabling them to interact with and respond to their environment, thus providing valuable data for various applications across industries.

5. Write short notes on the following. 4x5=20

(a) Actuators and its types
(b) MQTT, CoAP and XMPP 10T protocols
(c) Challenges of IoT
(d) Applications of fog computing

Ans:

(a) Actuators and Its Types

Actuators are devices that convert energy (often electrical) into physical motion or action. In IoT systems, actuators are used to control or move mechanisms or systems in response to a command. They are critical components in IoT, as they allow systems to interact with the physical world, making decisions and acting upon them.

Types of Actuators:

1. Electric Actuators:
Function: Convert electrical energy into mechanical motion.
Examples: Electric motors (AC or DC), solenoids.
Applications: Used in robotics, industrial automation, and household appliances (e.g., electric door locks).

2. Hydraulic Actuators:
Function: Use fluid pressure to create motion.
Examples: Hydraulic cylinders, pumps.
Applications: Heavy machinery, automotive systems (e.g., braking systems), and industrial equipment.

3. Pneumatic Actuators:
Function: Use compressed air to produce motion.
Examples: Pneumatic cylinders, air brakes.
Applications: Automation systems, material handling, and air-powered tools.

4. Thermal or Magnetic Actuators:
Function: Use heat or magnetic fields to induce movement.
Examples: Bimetallic strips, shape memory alloys.
Applications: Thermostats, temperature-sensitive switches, and magnetic relays.

5. Mechanical Actuators:
Function: Convert rotary or linear motion manually or via a mechanical input.
Examples: Gears, levers, cams.
Applications: Clocks, manual tools, and certain types of machinery.

(b) MQTT, CoAP, and XMPP IoT Protocols

MQTT (Message Queuing Telemetry Transport):
Overview: MQTT is a lightweight, publish-subscribe network protocol designed for constrained devices and low-bandwidth, high-latency networks.
Features:
- **Low Bandwidth Usage:** Ideal for IoT applications with limited network resources.
- **Publish-Subscribe Model:** Enables decoupling of message publishers and subscribers, allowing for scalable communication.
- **QoS Levels:** Provides different levels of Quality of Service (QoS) to ensure reliable message delivery.

Applications: Remote monitoring, smart home devices, and sensor networks.

CoAP (Constrained Application Protocol):
Overview: CoAP is a web transfer protocol designed for use with constrained nodes and networks in the IoT. It is similar to HTTP but optimized for low-power, lossy networks.
Features:
- **RESTful API:** Supports RESTful architecture, making it easy to integrate with web services.
- **Low Overhead:** Designed to work with devices that have limited processing power and memory.
- **Reliability:** Uses a lightweight message layer with optional reliability through acknowledgment.

Applications: Smart energy meters, home automation, and environmental monitoring.

XMPP (Extensible Messaging and Presence Protocol):
Overview: XMPP is a communication protocol for message-oriented middleware based on XML. It is designed for real-time communication and is used in instant messaging, presence information, and IoT applications.
Features:
- **Real-Time Communication:** Supports instant message delivery and presence updates.
- **Security:** Built-in support for encryption and secure communication.
- **Extensibility:** Highly extensible through the use of XML stanzas.

Applications: Real-time messaging in IoT, presence detection, and device-to-device communication.

(c) Challenges of IoT
1. Security and Privacy:
Challenge: IoT devices often lack robust security features, making them vulnerable to cyberattacks. Ensuring data privacy and secure communication between devices is critical but challenging due to resource constraints on IoT devices.
Example: IoT devices in smart homes can be hacked to access personal information or control the systems.
2. Interoperability:
Challenge: The diversity of IoT devices and communication protocols creates compatibility issues, making it difficult for devices from different manufacturers to work together seamlessly.
Example: Integrating devices from different vendors in a smart home system can be complex due to differing protocols.
3. Scalability:
Challenge: Managing and scaling an IoT network with potentially millions of devices is a significant challenge, particularly in terms of data storage, processing, and network management.
Example: Smart city projects require handling massive amounts of data generated by sensors, cameras, and other IoT devices.
4. Data Management:
Challenge: IoT generates vast amounts of data, requiring efficient storage, processing, and analysis. Managing this data while ensuring its integrity and accessibility is a challenge.
Example: IoT in healthcare produces large datasets that need to be processed in real-time for critical decision-making.
5. Energy Consumption:
Challenge: Many IoT devices are battery-powered, and minimizing energy consumption is essential to prolong device life and reduce maintenance costs.
Example: Sensors in remote locations need to operate for long periods without battery replacement.

(d) Applications of Fog Computing
Fog Computing is a decentralized computing infrastructure that extends cloud computing capabilities to the edge of the network. It processes data locally on edge devices or near the data source, reducing latency and bandwidth usage.

Applications:
1. Smart Cities:
Explanation: Fog computing is used in smart cities to process data from various sensors (e.g., traffic lights, surveillance cameras) locally, enabling real-time decision-making for traffic management, public safety, and energy efficiency.
Benefit: Reduces the need to send all data to a central cloud, which minimizes latency and enhances responsiveness.
2. Industrial IoT (IIoT):
Explanation: In industrial environments, fog computing processes data from machines and sensors on the factory floor, allowing for real-time monitoring, predictive maintenance, and process optimization.
Benefit: Ensures quick responses to anomalies, reducing downtime and improving operational efficiency.
3. Healthcare:
Explanation: Fog computing in healthcare enables real-time processing of data from wearable devices, medical sensors, and imaging equipment, allowing for immediate analysis and alerts for critical health conditions.
Benefit: Enhances patient care by providing real-time insights and reducing the latency associated with cloud processing.
4. Autonomous Vehicles:

Explanation: Fog computing is used in autonomous vehicles to process data from various sensors (e.g., LIDAR, cameras) locally, enabling real-time decision-making for navigation, obstacle detection, and vehicle control.
Benefit: Reduces latency and ensures that critical decisions are made without delay, which is essential for safety.
5. Retail:
Explanation: In retail environments, fog computing enables real-time analysis of customer data, inventory levels, and security footage, providing insights for personalized marketing, dynamic pricing, and loss prevention.
Benefit: Improves customer experience and operational efficiency by processing data at the edge.

These notes provide a concise overview of the key concepts, challenges, and applications related to actuators, IoT protocols, IoT challenges, and fog computing in the context of IoT.

IGNOU Cloud Computing and IoT Previous Years Solved Papers

Link:	https://www.youtube.com/playlist?list=PLzlh_31VWEFq5Z1ZlVFO1dbiSaifWzk7R
QR Code:	